TEXAS
CAKEWALK

TEXAS

CAKEWALK

True Crime Lynchings in Wyoming Territory 1889

Patricia Stinson

Published by Parchment Global Publishg

Printed in the United States of America
This book is creative non-fiction based on historical facts.
2024
First Edition

ISBN: 978-1-959483-57-1 (sc)
ISBN: 978-1-959483-58-8 (e)

Library of Congress Control Number: 2023907220

ACKNOWLEDGEMENTS

I could not have written this true crime story without the help and encouragement of Cobblestone Writers' Group.

A big debt of gratitude to Margaret Campbell, who was very patient in reading the manuscript, even parts of it over the phone during COVID.

And Jehovah, who would not let me rest until I wrote this story.

INTRODUCTION

My dear reader,

Texas Cakewalk is a phrase used for a lynching in the 1800s.

This book is historical fiction. There are eight main characters. Each person lived in the 1840s.

The main characters of this true crime story lived and worked in Casper, Rawlins, Cheyenne, and the prairies of the Wyoming Territory in the 1880s.

This book contains mini stories featuring one of the eight main characters and their coming together in their pursuit of what they wanted.

Each person is profiled as accurately as my research took me. They were people who loved, laughed and struggled. They were human and even the best of them had flaws but also virtues. Each had his or her own identity. Motives and personalities are as I saw from my research.

This is part non-fiction in that the eight main characters, seven men and one woman, lived and came together in one historical event. It is fiction in the dialogue, as I was not there more than one hundred years ago, despite what my gray hair may imply, and a few minor characters.

The background of each character influenced their decisions and actions. They all faced difficulties and opportunities. Each felt he was independent, unknowing they were manipulated.

I portray six men who left their past behind and became rich cattle men. The men were Albert John Bothwell, Robert B. Conner. Tom Soleil (aka Tom Sun), Robert M. Galbraith, John Henry Durbin and Ernest McLean.

I portray two people who left their past behind and became small ranchers and farmers, aka nesters. They were James (Jim, Jimmy) Averell and Ellen Watson.

The characters came from different backgrounds, but they collided at an historic time in the Wyoming Territory.

CHAPTER ONE

"Hey kid, I'll give you two-bits to watch my mule and horse while I get some tonsil paint. If anyone tries to steal them, come into the saloon, and tell me."

A grubby boy in stained cotton pants and shirt stopped and eyed the man. The grizzled old man, wearing rugged black leather pants, under his leather hunting shirt, and a turban hat made of a big bandanna, which covered the top of his long, dirty hair, was standing in front of the St. Louis groggery.

Crossing the wide, dusty street by dodging horses, and mules pulling drays and carriages and several piles of horse dung, he stepped onto a narrow boardwalk in front of the saloon.

"Shur, mister. If I steal them and come and tell you someone else stole your outfit, what then?" the boy asked as he grinned.

1

"I'd hand you your guts after I slit you open." The man grinned, showing yellow and brown teeth.

The boy smiled. "Okay, I'll keep an eye on your trappin's. Hey, what's your name?"

"Folks call me Dakota. What's yours?"

"Folks call me Tom DeBeau Soleil."

"Let's just make it Tom Soleil." After a wink and a grin, Dakota stepped into the bar.

Shade provided by the building made it the best place to sit and keep an eye on the animals. A breeze swept up the dusty street as Tom sat in the dirt and listened to his grumbling stomach.

Three hours later, the bat-wing doors of the hootch house opened and Dakota flipped a coin to Tom. "You did fine. You kept your word and stayed here." He walked over to his bay.

"Dakota, where are you goin'? I see you packed your mule with supplies."

"Goin' cross the Mississip. I trap for beaver furs. Make it to St. Louis every three or four years."

"Will you be goin' near Montana? I've an uncle there I want to make acquaintance with."

"Might be eventually. Where are your people?"

"My ma died, and pa married a mean woman. He has to put up with her as he's hitched to her, but I ain't, so I left."

"So, you be a guttersnipe. How old are you?"

"Yes sir, I'm eleven."

"Where do you hale from?"

"Canada. I got me a mule. Figured my pa owed me that much, him getting' married to such a hag."

"Reckon, it's okay. Do as I say, or I'll leave ya wherever we be. I'll stake you to provisions, and you can pay me back after you learn how to trap for yourself. You can ride your mule."

"Deal." Tom flashed a smile.

"Come on, if you're comin'."

*　　*　　*

Wading into the shallow water near the pond's tree line, Tom thrust a pole through the ring on the beaver trap to open the mouth and mark the placement. He placed a willow twig over the trap with one end in the pond bottom and one in the crown slightly below the water surface. After securing the trap, he smeared the beaver scent he got from the glands of earlier catches on the exposed part of the willow switch. The musky odor drifted in the air until he put a plug-stopper back into the bottle made of buffalo horn. After working and living with Dakota for several years, he was confident in his skills and did not waste time.

After setting his eighth and last trap, he retraced his way to the campsite he had with Dakota.

His partner was stretching his pelts over willow frames to dry. Without a word, Tom laid the drowned beavers he had collected during the day by a tree and began skinning their hides.

"Took you longer than usual. What delayed you?" asked Dakota.

"An Arapaho brave took a beaver from one of my traps. Had to track him down."

"Did you catch him?"

"I got the beaver back. The brave won't be needin' it."

"Good. You've got to keep what is yours. Fight for it if need be." Dakota eyed his stack of beaver pelts and compared it to Tom's The same. Each man had his personal mark on his hides. Smiling, he put an iron pot half full of river water over the low fire. "After you shot the deer this morning, hung, and bled it, I cut out the heart, liver, and kidneys. I pulled out the bile bladder so the liver and kidneys can be boiled and the heart I'll roast. We will have a tongue-licking' supper tonight. I'll save the fat from the kidneys for making pemmican later. I'll cook while you skin the deer and cut up the meat."

Tom nodded.

* * *

"Seems like a fair spot to hunker down for the night." Dakota reined his horse into the shade of a tree.

"Early, ain't it?" Tom halted his horse.

"Yep, but my bones say this is a top-notch spot by the stream. You gut the rabbits and raccoon and get the hides ready to cure while I start a fire." Dakota eased off his horse.

Tom, taller than Dakota and a younger-looking version, put his hands on the withers and jumped from his horse. He threw the dead animals to the side. "Uh-ha. But first, I'll unsaddle the broncs and stake them out to graze near the river while you gather the wood for the fire." Tom noticed Dakota's swollen knuckles, and knew his partner's joints ached, although he never said a word. *He is crippled from working in the cold river water and staying in the mountains in the winter. Likely, I'll be the same if I keep doing this. I've got to think of my future. I have to go on my own and leave our partnership.* Tom's thoughts tumbled in his head as he staked out the horses to graze.

Not long after Tom returned to the campsite he handed the rabbit meat to Dakota, who slid it onto a sharpened stick and hung the skewer over the fire. With his skinning blade, Tom worked on the raccoon and rabbit pelts.

Dakota kept watching the meat. "Tom, we been trappin' together for six or seven years now, I figure. You know all I can teach you about trappin', huntin', and survivin'. We never got to Montana."

"Yup."

"Got me a notion of spendin' the winter in St. Louis. My bones don't hanker for the icy winds and snow with just cabin shelter anymore. You be welcome to come with me. Or might be, you still be interested in findin' your uncle."

The skinning blade stopped for a moment and then continued dislodging the fat from the fur's inside. "Don't need to now. I can care for myself. I'd like to join the army, but I'm too young. Last month, when we sold some pelts at the fort, I heered tell there was construction work in Oklahoma where the army wants to build another fort. I've pondered on things, and it's the place for me to learn somethin' else besides trappin'. Maybe I can scout for the army. Don't think there is an age requirement for that."

Dakota smiled and nodded his head. "Hear you. I was your age once. I didn't want to sit around in a tenderfoot place. Wanted the outdoors. But trappin' doesn't make as much as it did."

Still working with the knife, Tom replied, "I love these mountains. Ain't nothin' better, in my mind. After the War Between the States, I'll likely be comin' back to these parts."

A skewed hunk of meat hanging over the fire let drops of blood fall into the flames. The fire sputtered, and the sparks flew into the air. Dakota turned the skewer as he said, "Well, you're gritty enough for it." A wide grin spread out under his beard and mustache.

The following day, Tom stood and extended his hand to Dakota. "I'm beholding to you. You taught me how to survive and fight for what I want. You made me strong with grit. Without you, I'd likely have ended up as a gutter rat. You were better than my real pa." Tom's serious look in his eyes told him he was saying the truth.

Dakota shook Tom's hand and said, "You've been like a son to me. Hope the best for you."

"I'm giving you ten of my beaver hides to thank you and you got to take them or I'll feel right bad," said Tom.

"I hear you, Son. And thank ye." Dakota shook hands with Tom again as his near toothless smile flashed for a moment.

Tom and Dakota parted ways. Dakota headed for warmth and civilization, while Tom headed for Oklahoma, scouting, construction, surveying, and a new beginning.

Note: Dakota's name was Descoteaux. He was a mountain man and lived with Native tribes at times. He hunted beavers. He met Tom in St. Louis and taught him the mountain man life.

CHAPTER TWO

"Hey, Tom, wait up," shouted Scout Boney Earnest.

Tom stopped walking across Fort Fred Steele's drill ground. With straight forward strides in his knee-high leather moccasins, he turned and walked to Boney, who was stepping off the boardwalk in front of Captain Anson Mills's office.

When the men met, Boney said, "Captain Mills says we two are his best scouts at the fort, and he wants us to track some Arapahos who attacked a group of hunters. They killed the men and took their wives."

"Why not Bill Cody?" asked Tom.

"He is out scouting on another matter."

"Where do we start? "asked Tom.

"In Yellowstone country. We're familiar with the area since we've been out that way before. The captain is sending out a burial detail. We will go with them as they know where the campsite is. While the troopers bury the men and bring back any personal property, we'll try to pick up a trail and follow the hoofprints," said Scout Boney. "Once we locate the wives, one of us can come back and alert the cavalry."

"What are we waiting for?" Tom strode to the horse barn.

*   *   *

The two men packed jerky, water bags, ammunition, and oats for the mustangs. They saddled and rode out the fort's gate shortly after high sun, along with the troopers sent to bury the hunters.

For a mile the broncs trotted down a hard-packed dirt path and then branched off across land with sand, rough mesquite, and scraggly grassy patches. When the horses began huffing and sweating, the men slowed them to a walk to rest them and after a time, back to a trot. Later, they stopped to let the animals rest at the shallow creek branching off the Big Horn River.

For the rest of the day, the troopers rode on the hot, dry land. At sunset, the detail found the campsite. The two scouts told the burial detail to stay back while they dismounted and walked around the area, looking for the marauding Indians' signs. They scoured the land, spied some partial hoof prints, and followed them for a half-mile. They walked while leading the horses back and released the burial squad to do its work. Scattered on the ground, men's scalped, twisted bodies, women's clothing and tools littered the area. Coyotes and vultures had done their work on the bloody bodies. With flies swarming, the burial crew set up their camp and began their work. All the men knew the weapons and horses would be gone.

The scouts cold camped away from the site until sunup, taking turns as night guards. With the first rays, they mounted and followed the tracks, as there had been no effort to obliterate them. They trotted up a slight elevation, and then the land became steeper, and their horses worked harder. The men got off and led their mounts up the steep incline. Finally, the land flattened out, filled with scrub trees and patches of grass.

Midafternoon, Boney and Tom dismounted. Slapping their hats against their legs, they shook the sand and dust off them. They poured water into their Stetsons from the water bags, and offered the drink to their mounts, who slurped the water greedily.

"Boney, I'm thinking of asking Mary Agnas the sergeant's daughter to marry me. She is a good worker, never slacks off, she is used to the life out here, and she is passable in the looks department." Taking the bandana from his neck, he wiped his sweaty hair plastered against his forehead.

RATTLE. RATTLE. The sound pierced through the hot air.

Tom knew what the sound meant. Don't move!

Crack!

Tom jumped back. "Devil-ding."

Holstering his pistol, Boney stepped forward. "Did I kill it?"

"You did. Almost took its head off. Thanks." At his feet lay the dead rattlesnake. Tom picked the serpent up and wrapped it in his neck scarf before stuffing it into his saddlebag.

"What do you want that for?"

"Dunno. It may come in handy. Never know. Besides, snake meat is toothsome," Tom said, as the two men mounted and put their horses into a trot.

After halting a few hours at night to rest the geldings, they continued to travel. An almost full moon in a cloudless sky lit their way, so they kept going forward.

Deep into the night, Tom stopped. "Smell that?"

"Sure do. Let's walk," said Boney.

Leading their horses, they moved forward, staring at the ground. Boney stopped and pointed with his boot toe. "Fresh horse droppings."

The men hobbled their horses and crawled forward in a crouched position. Tom tapped his nose. Boney nodded. The slight trace of pungent smoke wafted in the air and assailed their nostrils. Clouds had come in and scudded across the ebony sky and covered the moon, making the night as black as a grizzly bear's den.

They felt their way to a rise in rocks guided by their noses. The clouds drifted past the moon, and the night lit up like candlelight. Staying below the ridge so they would not be seen against the sky, they laid on their bellies and peered around a boulder.

Five women, visible in the camp's firelight, huddled together on one side. Their wrists and ankles tied them to each other. Arapahos sat near the fire, eating by slicing meat off of the small animal hanging on a spit over the fire.

Tom tapped Boney's shoulder. He flashed five fingers three times, then one to signal sixteen Arapaho braves.

Boney nodded. Tapping Tom's arm, he pointed to the left side of the camp.

Tom nodded.

Crawling across the grit and jagged stones for several yards, they came to a stand of birch trees. In the night shadows, they saw the Indian ponies. They crept to the tethering ropes, working silently; they untied five. The scouts led them further away from the campsite for several minutes before doubling back to where they had left their horses and hobbled the Arapaho ponies next to theirs. After securing the five extra horses, Tom took the dead rattlesnake in his hand. In a silent crouched position, they crept back to the rest of the Arapahos' herd, untied them, and waved their arms and Stetsons in the air. The mustangs nodded their heads, snorted, and milled about. Tom picked up some sand and threw it in the air, so it rained down on the animals while he shook the rattler's tail. The ponies took off at a gallop.

Alarmed, the Arapahos stood at the sound of the commotion.

Yelling, they left the women and ran to the trees.

Boney and Tom smiled and sprinted toward the women.

"Help us. Save us." The women sobbed.

Tom and Boney motioned them to be quiet. "Quiet! All of you! Shut up!" Tom commanded in a whisper. "Sit still and be quiet while we slit the leather ropes binding your hands and feet to each other. When everyone is free, follow us and don't make a sound. Bring the ties."

"Why?" asked a quivering voice in the night.

"Hush-up."

Boney and Tom drew their knives from their leg sheathes and set to work removing the women's bindings, which were cutting into their ankles and wrists.

"Follow me," whispered Boney under his breath.

The freed captives followed Boney up the hill on their cut and bruised bare feet as he led the women to their horses.

As he freed the broncs, Tom whispered. "Can any of you ride bareback?"

"I can. I rode our farm horse when I was a girl." Another woman said, "I can ride."

"This will be different from riding a plow horse, but you have some idea. Boney will help you two mount two of the Indian ponies. Two, who don't know how to ride, will use our saddled mounts. Boney and I will ride two Indian ponies."

Tom walked over to the teenage sobbing girl. "You are lightweight, so you can ride the last horse. Boney or I will ride beside you and keep you on."

He helped her mount. "Here, stuff this into your mouth to muffle your sobbing," he said as he lifted the hem of her dress and thrust it into her hand.

Linking the horses together with the leather thongs, they walked the geldings away from the rise.

The women gripped the manes.

"Can't we go faster?" A voice in the dark drifted up the line.

"Make too much noise. We will later. No palaver," Tom's voice showed his aggravation. Later, he dropped back to see if the Arapahos were following. He roped sagebrush and pulled it over the ground behind the retreating bunch to cover their tracks. An hour later, he caught up with the group.

Putting the horses into a slow trot, Boney and Tom kept an eye on the women to steady any that looked like they were going to tumble off. Later, they slowed to a walk.

One of the older women rode next to Boney. "My name is Sarah. Do you think the Indians will come after us?" They could catch up with us easily."

Boney answered, "We put a dead rattler by the cayuses. They will think a rattler spooked their horses before one pony trampled him to death. They will go after their ponies, and as we took five ponies for you women to ride, they will continue to look for their mounts. Warriors put a lot of stock in their horses. When they see you are missing, they will think you would not make it far. As we brought the leather ties, they will search for you after they find their horses."

"I hope so. I want this nightmare to be over," said Sarah.

Under the shelter of a broad outcropping of rocks, they stopped for rest. The females slid off and collapsed onto the gritty sand and stones. The youngest had stopped crying. She lay exhausted on the ground. Tom and Boney passed around the canteens of water.

Before daylight, they began again. As the day went on, the women became better at riding.

Boney and Tom took turns dropping back to see if the Arapahos followed them. Each time, the scout would return and say, "So far, no sign of them."

They stayed in the shadows, which the cliffs stretched across the valley. By noon, they stopped by a small tree shaded creek. Everyone dismounted. The exhausted and suffering widows sat on the water's edge, soaked their feet and cupped their hands to draw up water to drink and wash their faces.

After an hour's rest, Boney announced, "Okay, everyone. Get back on the ponies. We need to start."

"We can't. We're too worn out. We need to rest longer," said the youngest woman.

"If you gals don't mount the horses, Boney and I will have no choice but to leave you here for the Arapahos. We don't want them to capture us. We stole their horses. They are riled up. So, get up or stay here without us," said Tom.

The women struggled up, and the men helped them mount the horses. Tom brought up the rear, and Boney dropped back and whispered, "Tom, did you mean what you said?"

"Doesn't matter if I meant it or not. It worked, didn't it?"

Just before sundown, they arrived at the fort. All five widows slid off and collapsed on the ground, sobbing with relief inside the gate. The army surgeon rushed out to them and had them taken to the small infirmary while Boney and Tom stabled their horses.

"Sure am glad you were with me to fetch the women. You know how the Indians think and how to survive. Don't think I could have done it my ownself." Boney removed the bit from his horse and put on its halter. "You sure were determined out there."

"To live out here, one needs to know how to survive and do whatever is necessary to do it. Those hunters were idiots to bring their wives out here when they couldn't take care of them. I aim to marry and have a family and I ain't going to put them in danger. We'll live in a civilized place. A place with land, mountains and towns," said Tom as he brushed his horse's flank. "And no one is taking what is mine."

"Good luck on finding that."

"Don't need luck, just doin'."

*   *   *

Five months later, Tom slid the saddle blanket on his gelding's withers and pulled it back to its place for the saddle. Satisfied the hairs on the horse's back would be in the same direction, he gently placed the saddle on it. As he reached under the horse's belly to grab the cinch, Boney walked into the stable.

"Goin' someplace, Tom?" asked Boney.

"Wyoming Territory. It's time to plant my feet permanently while I'm strong to do the hard work. Goin' to scout for the railroad. Learn me some surveying and building. Mary Agnes said she is willing to marry me when I find our future home." He finished saddling his mount, tied his bedroll, and extra blanket behind the saddle, and walked the horse out of the barn. Mounting, he looked down at Boney. "Agreeable riding with you." Without waiting, he neck-reined and rode out the fort gate. "Might see you again," he called back over his shoulder.

CHAPTER THREE

Mud splattered onto his trousers as the horse jogged by on the muddy street. A clump hit him in the face. His sleeved arm wiped it off as he walked past one of the twenty-five tent saloons in the town of Benton. Loud voices filled the bars. The fist fights and gun fights started in the saloons, often gorged out into the thick mud-covered street. Drunken men streamed in and out of the five tent brothels.

Reaching his tent office, Robert Galbraith sighed in relief he had made it safely to the railroad yard. He sat on a rickety wooden chair by a table scarred by knife cuts. He heard the shooting of guns coming from the town of Benton and hoped a stray bullet would not find him. *They call this town Hell On Wheels. A perfect name for this place.* Galbraith's thoughts were interrupted by a visitor.

"Hey, Galbraith, how much longer before we move on?" said an unshaved man carrying a rifle as he stepped into the railroad's manager's tent.

"By the end of the week, Tom. The track has been laid all the way to thirty miles from here. So, we will pull up stakes and move to the new site to extend the rails. It can't be soon enough for me." "Do you think the saloons and cathouses will come to the new site? asked the scout, Tom Soleil.

"I imagine so. At least we will be further away from Fort Fred Steele, so the off-duty soldiers aren't likely to swarm in and it may discourage the gold prospectors as well. Then it will be just our railroad workers to contend with."

"Yeah, I bet a hundred men are killed on a weekend, the way bodies are stacked up." Tom Soleil shifted his weight.

"When we get closer to Cheyenne, I'm quitting the railroad and starting a cattle ranch. There's lots of land for grazing and the army forts and settlers need beef." Mr. Galbraith shuffled the papers on his table desk.

"I aim the same as you. I'm going to get some land in the Wyoming Territory, not too far from Cheyenne. I got a lady spoken for and I aim to have me a cattle ranch and be my own boss."

"You're French Canadian, aren't you?"

"Yeah."

"Only folks born in the U.S. are allowed to homestead. To get away with filing on a property, you will have to change your name and place of birth."

"Hadn't thought of that." Tom looked out the tent flap door. Wagons rolled by, and men with sledge hammers milled about.

Heat waves came up from the ground and disappeared in the sunlight. "Sun. Tom Sun will be an easy name to remember."

Robert Galbraith smiled. "And where were you born, Tom Sun?"

"Some place back East. Know of any likely spots?"

"I hear Vermont is a pretty Union state."

"So that's it. I'm Tom Sun from the state of Vermont." The two men smiled.

"After I stake a claim and build a place for Mary Agnas, I aim to go to the Black Hill and look for gold. I hope to find enough to start my cattle ranch in a big way. I reckon small ranches won't make it. Too many things can go wrong with the rustlers, draughts and life in general," said Tom.

"Watch out Gold Fever doesn't get you. Some men can't quit looking for yellow sand. And other prospectors will jump a paying claim. You could wind up dead," said Robert Galbraith.

"I ain't afeered. I had a wise mountain man for a teacher. He taught me to get what I go after. I'll keep my aim on the ranch. Well, I best earn my pay and hunt up some meat for the stew pot. The men eat a lot and don't like being short shifted on the dinner plate. They take it out on the cook, and he comes after me. See you later." Tom walked through the tent door flap and headed for his horse. "But first I'm goin' to watch a mob hang a fella called Dutch. It might be interestin'."

"What did he do?"

Tom said, "Don't know. But they're given him a Texas Cakewalk for somethin'."

Galbraith called out, "I sure hope you know what you are doing about the gold prospecting. Good luck. You'll need it."

ELLEN

CHAPTER FOUR

She heard his boot step on the wood plank outside the cabin door. Ellen moved back toward the corner near the back door.

The front door swung open, banging against the wall. He staggered in and blinked in the lantern light with a dazed look. "Where's my supper?"

"You didn't come home for supper. It's after ten o'clock."

"Woman, you're to have my supper ready when I say it's time. Now is the time. First, go out and put my horse in the barn. Now." He took a flask from his overalls back pocket.

"Bill, maybe you should eat before you drink anymore." Ellen edged away from her position. She followed the side wall, hoping to get past him and out the door.

"You can't boss me around. I'll drink whenever I want. I'm your husband, and you do what I say." He reached out and caught Ellen in a tight grip. Putting the flask down, he slapped her repeatedly across the face, on the side of her head, and yanked on her hair.

She tried to push him away, but he held onto her hair. She stamped on his boots, but they were so thick he barely felt it.

"How dare you try to fight me?" Still holding Ellen by her hair, he pulled her over to a wall and took down a short whip. "I'm going to teach you to not even dare to fight me, if I need to skin you alive." He raised the whip and brought it down hard on his wife, then he raised his arm and whip and brought it down again.

After the third blow and despite the intense pain, Ellen turned her head and raised it as high as she could. She bit down on his arm just above the hand holding the whip.

Howling in pain, he pushed her away and dropped the whip.

She grabbed a table chair and brought it down on his head with all her might. Dropping the pieces of the shattered chair, she ran out the door. She tripped on a plank on the porch and sprawled on the ground. She looked back and saw Bill lying on the floor, holding a hunk of her hair in his grip.

She got up and ran across the plowed field. The night was black as a deep cave. Hoping she was going in the right direction, she ran until she felt her lungs would burst. She fell to her knees and looked back, but the tar-pitch night made it impossible to see if he was coming after her. After taking several breaths, she got up and started running. A few minutes later, she saw a glimmer of light moving slowly. *That's Poppa leaving the barn and going to the house. Please, Poppa, don't blow the lantern out.* Running and staggering, she kept staring at the light. An eternity later, she saw the dark outline of the barn and house. She stumbled to the short wooden porch in front of the house door and burst in.

Startled, parents and siblings stared at the door. "Ellen!" They rushed forward.

"Poppa, help me."

"Yes. Yes. Of course. What has happened? You look awful. Is Bill all right?"

Her mother held her as they walked to a chair. Ellen sat and began sobbing.

"It's Bill. I can't go back to him. I can't. He'll kill me."

*   *   *

"Now, you are no longer Mrs. Ellen Pickell, and your divorce is final; do you want to stay on the farm and help your momma and me? I'm buying an adjacent farm. There is plenty of work to do." Mr. Watson took the pitchfork and tossed hay into the stall. Ellen set two buckets of milk by the barn door.

"No, Poppa. You'll have plenty of help from by brothers and sisters. I'm Ellen Watson now and I want to make my own way. No more marriage for me and having to depend on a man. I want to get a job in Red Cloud and earn money, so I can go by train to Cheyenne, Wyoming. I heard it's a growing city, and I think I can get a job there as a cook or housekeeper." Ellen picked up a water bucket and took it to a stall.

"Cheyenne! That's too far from your home here in Kansas. We'll not see you." Mr. Watson stopped pitching hay and leaned on the pitch fork.

"I can write letters. It will be good, Poppa."

Mr. Watson sighed. "I see you are stubborn and determined to go. But, you remember, if things go wrong, you can always come home to you poppa and momma."

*   *   *

Ellen set three vinegar pies on a long table by the open window. She gathered up the bowls and pans to place in the dry sink. The corner of her eye caught sight of a child's hands grabbing a pie. She rushed to the window and saw a boy running down the alley where another boy joined him, and they ran off.

I've seen those rascals about town. I'm going to track them down right this minute. Ellen took off her apron and went out the back door of the restaurant kitchen.

She strode down the alley and went to the next alley. Barrels and crates littered both sides. She saw a bare foot sticking out between the crates. Marching to the boxes, she found two young boys stuffing their faces with pie.

Their eyes widened in horror. "We're sorry. Honest, we're sorry," said the younger child.

"Yeah, lady. We're just hungry, that's all. The pie was all we found to eat. You won't take us to the sheriff, will you?" said the older boy.

Ellen glared at the boys with her hands on her hips. "Where do you boys live?"

"Nowhere."

"Where's your ma and pa?"

"My ma ran off, and pa sweeps up and empties the spittoon for drinks in the saloon. His ma," the older boy pointed to the younger one, "works at the bawdy house, and she doesn't want him hanging around. We sleep where we can and scrounge for food."

The younger boy said, "You gonna have the sheriff put us in jail?"

"What're your names?"

"My name is John DeCorey, and this is Gene Crowder," said the older boy.

"Well, now, that pie costs money. Do you have any?"

"No, Mam." Both boys looked down at their sticky hands and pieces of the crumbled pie in their laps.

"Nothing else to do. You two will have to come with me and work it off." Ellen began walking back down the alley.

"You mean, you ain't gonna set the sheriff on us?" said the younger boy, Gene.

"Nope, not if you work it off."

The two boys jumped up and ran after Ellen.

Ellen noticed Gene was limping. "What happened to your leg?"

"When I went into the saloon to speak to my ma, her friend picked me up and threw me out the door. My leg broke and it didn't heal right."

Ellen closed her eyes for a moment and bit her lower lip. "Well, times a wasting. We got work to do."

CHAPTER FIVE

Land to Goshen, Jimmy Averell! You just got discharged on May 22 in Mississippi. You're out of the military for less than a month, and you want to re-enlist in June? Haven't you had enough?"

"The army life has been good for me, Sister Sarah," said James.

Sarah sighed. Shaking her head, she said, "I suppose the infantry in 1876 is better than during the Civil War. If that is what you want, you should do it."

"Thanks Sarah, and I'll come and say goodbye to Able and you and that nephew of mine. Ralph is a great kid." James Averell kissed his sister on the forehead before leaving to re-enlist.

* * *

Three years later, in 1879, James Averell, promoted to Sergeant, was stationed at Fort McKinney near Buffalo in the Wyoming Territory.

Jim opened the door of Mrs. O'Dell's pleasure palace and, after looking at the customers, he entered. He went up to a soldier he knew was on leave for the weekend. "Hi, private, how's it going?"

"Great. Two days off and my pay in my pocket."

"One drink for me. I'm not staying long. I own a house in town which I rent out. I'm going to stay there tonight. I don't want to run into a guy named Charlie Johnson. He is a mean son-of -a-gun. He says I insulted him and wants to get even," said Jim Averell.

The private noticed the smiling women wearing thick make-up waiting for someone to sit and buy them a drink. A couple men were drinking and laughing with two women at a corner table.

"Think I'll stay awhile," said the private.

After the men put the money on the bar and James turned to leave, the bat-winged doors banged open.

"I seen the army saddles on the broncs outside, and I figured you were in here," bellowed a burly man who lunged through the doors.

The room became quiet, and everyone looked at Johnson and Averill. The Sargeant drew his revolver. "Stay back, Charlie. Don't be a lunk head. I don't want to fight."

"Lunk head. You calling me names?" Charlie Johnson jerked his head back and glowered at Averill's gun. "Put up your pistol; I'm going to beat the tar out of you. You're a cowardly no good. I'll fix your flint, that's for dang sure. " Charlie lunged forward.

Sergeant Averill fired his pistol into the roof. "Stand back, Charlie, and don't call me names again. I won't stand for it."

Charlie took a step forward. Jim fired downward. The bullet hit Charlie in the left leg. Johnson wheeled around, and before he could spin back to face Jim, a third shot hit him in the back.

A huge gasp from the onlookers conflicted with the sound of the gun. Charlie fell on the sawdust floor with a heavy thud.

A man sitting at the corner table drinking with a woman stood. "Charlie's my friend. You shot him in the back. I'm gonna get him into a hotel room and find a doctor, and don't you try to stop me," said Frank Murphy as he threw a chair aside.

Jim Averill nodded.

*   *   *

The streets of Rawlins were busy with wagons, mules, horses, and shoppers. The raucous sound of a hammer hitting an anvil at the blacksmith's shop added to the din.

"Hey, Jim Rankin." A man in a black frock coat sprinted up to Jim.

"Yep, Justice McAllen. You want to see me?" Sheriff Jim Rankin opened the jailhouse door. The two men entered the small office where Bob Rankin, Jim's brother, sat behind a desk.

"Yes, I do. It took Charlie Johnson eight days to do it, but he died. Even though he was a brawler and drunkard with a long police record, and he got away with killing McLeod, he was shot in the back, so we need to hold a grand jury meeting into this matter. It happened in Buffalo, but the hearing will be here in the county seat of Rawlins." While he was talking, the judge shook hands with the jailer, Bob Rankin. "Because you're the sheriff of the county and your brother Bob, is the jailer here I need you to bring in Sargeant James Averill from Buffalo as soon as you can. I hear you three are friends Will that be a problem?"

"Not a problem for me. Don't know if it is for Jim. But I'll bring him in. That's for sure."

*   *   *

"Glad you're willing to come into the jail here in Rawlins and await the hearing, Jim." Sheriff Jim Rankin walked Sergeant Jim Averill to the cell door, closed it and turned the key.

"I know I'll get a fair deal. Rosa is cooking the meals, isn't she?"

"She sure is. By the way. I should warn you that an inmate from the territorial prison in Laramie, accused of murdering two police officers, will come here to stand trial. His name is George Parrott. He's nickname is Big Nose. He is vicious. I'll put him at the other end of the row of cells. He'll arrive next week, and his trial will be the day after he gets here. The Laramie prison houses him now for his other crimes. He's a cutthroat. It would be great to send him back. I want to get rid of him."

"Don't worry about me. You won't get any trouble from me," said the sergeant.

"Thanks, Jim."

*   *   *

The judge banged the gavel after he sat at his table. Everyone in the crowded courtroom sat. The room was quiet with expectancy. The trial had taken less than three hours, witnesses had testified, and the jury had deliberated and returned with a verdict within eighteen minutes after they got the case to consider.

"George Parrott stand."

Nig Nose, with shackles on his feet and hands, stood with the sheriff next to him.

"George Parrott, you have been found guilty of two first degree murders of two police officers. The court sentences you to die by hanging on April 2, 1881. Let the record show the sentence was pronounced on December 15, 1880. You will remain in the Jail until the day of the execution. The court is adjourned." The judge banged the gavel.

Spectators jumped, cheered, pounded each other on the back, and shook hands. Laughing and cheering rang in Big Nose's ears as he shuffled back to his jail cell.

*   *   *

Big Nose listened. The row of cells was quiet except for the buzzing of a few flies. His thick, handmade shackles clanked whenever he moved his feet or hands. *It isn't bad enough they lock me up in this tiny cell, but they keep me shackled all the time. Well, I have a few tricks up my sleeve.*

He inched his hands to his right-hand pocket. Feeling a slight bump, he pressed his fingers under the hidden pen knife pushing on the outside of the cloth and pushed up and kept pushing until a blade section popped above the pocket line. He pulled it out and had his penknife in his hand. He opened it and began sawing on the thick leather wrist bands that held metal links constricting his hands. After hours and hours of sawing back and forth, with his fingers cramping, a leather cuff connected to the metal linking the two cuffs separated. His eyes lit up like fire, and a smirk covered his face. Sitting on his cot, he waited.

Jailer Bob Rankin opened the door at the end of the hall with the cell keys. His wife Rosa followed behind with plates of biscuits and beans. They stopped first at Jim Averill's cell. Jailer Rankin unlocked the door, and Rosa went in with a plate.

"Oh, Rosa, that smells delicious. This was biscuit baking day, wasn't it?"

"Sure was. Enjoy."

"I surely will do that. Thank you, Rosa."

Rosa left the cell, and her husband locked the door. They walked down to the end of the hallway. They stopped at Big Nose's cell.

"Rosa, you stay out here. I'll take the food in." Bob unlocked the door and stepped inside with a plate of food.

Big Nose jumped and began pounding Bob with the heavy cuffs still on his wrist. He clubbed Bob over and over until the jailer fell to the floor senseless. The cell keys flew from his hands and landed on the floor in the hallway at Rosa's feet.

"Bob, Bob," shouted Rosa. Eyes wide with shock and fear, she grabbed the keys, closed the door, and locked it. "Bob, hang on." She ran down the hallway and into the street, screaming. "Help! Help! He's killing my husband. Help!"

All the men and women in the street and shops heard Rosa's screams. Rushing to her, they saw her pointing to the jail. "Help, Bob."

The women gathered around Rosa and stayed with her. The men bolted to the jail, some with their guns drawn. They went to the cell, and pointing their weapons forced Big Nose to go back into a corner while they dragged Bob out and then relocked the cell. The men carried the unconscious jailer to the doctor. With several stitches in his head and a giant headache, he was home by nightfall.

*   *   *

The townspeople chattered about the escape attempt throughout the following day. By evening, the men who gathered in the saloon mumbled about justice might not happen if Big Nose should escape.

"Hey, Jackson, my friends and I don't think the jail will be able to keep Big Nose until next April. That is a long way off. What do you say?" A man at the bar called out to a man entering the saloon.

"Sam, I didn't know you had any friends."

The men laughed, including Sam.

"I think the two Rankins are good men and can handle most prisoners. But Big Nose is something different. Outraged folks took care of his partner last year. A lynch mob gave him a Texas Cakewalk by stringing him up to a telegraph pole in Benton," said Jackson.

"I say, we'll go together and show Big Nose a Texas Cakewalk. The same justice his partner got last year. We'll have to get past both Rankin brothers. So, no one harms the Rankins. Agree?" Sam put down his beer.

"Agreed!" Loud voices erupted as the men finished their drinks and stampeded out the door.

The crowd marched across and down two streets, shouting, "Death! Death to the killer."

Feet stomping on the wood floor area before the jailhouse door, the men behind pushed the ones in front through the unlocked front door. Bob and Jim Rankin, on hearing the mob, stood as the men rushed through the entrance. The sheriff drew his gun and Bob grabbed a rifle from the wall.

"Men, you don't want to do this. Don't make me shoot anyone. You are all good men. I don't want anyone to get hurt," said the sheriff.

Men kept pushing their way into the small office. Before the sheriff could react, six men grabbed the brothers, disarmed them and held their arms behind them. Sam grabbed the keys on the wall peg, and the men went through the door to the cells.

Jackson yelled, Don't worry, Averill, we're not after you."

Jim, standing by the bars on his cell, gaped at the mob rushing past the cells and storming down the hallway.

Yelling and shouting, the mob jostled each other on their way to Big Nose's cell. They found him crouched back in a corner. Sam opened the cell, and seven men pushed in. Grabbing Big Nose, they shoved him out into the crowded hallway and down the gauntlet of angry vigilantes.

Bob and Jim Rankin were shoved and locked into the cell. "We'll let you out when we finish with our business," said a member of the lynching party.

"Yeah, we know you would try to stop us, but we're going to have justice our way," said another vigilante.

Out in the street, they half-carried Big Nose by his arms as he dragged his feet and struggled.

"You can't do this. I've got rights. You have to wait until April. This is wrong." Big Nose spit, yelled and cursed as he tried to dig in his heels.

At the railroad depot, they took him to a telegraph pole. His handcuffs had not been replaced, so his hands were free. Four men held onto his hands as others put a hemp rope around his neck and threw the other end around the wood arm sticking perpendicular from the pole.

"Don't strangle me. Please, I beg you. This is not a hangman's noose. It won't break my neck. I'll strangle slowly. Please have mercy." Big Nose's legs shook so he could not stand.

The mob put him up on a barrel and then kicked it from under him. His six feet two-inch height helped his feet to touch the ground.

"Dell-dang and Tarnation!" Jackson ran off and brought back a ladder. He leaned it against the pole and shortened the rope.

Big Nose, forced up the rungs, said, "You can't do this! Mercy! This is murder." He sobbed the words over and over. When he was halfway, Jackson yanked the ladder aside. George dangled . His massive arms wrapped around the pole. The heavy shackles still around his feet kept him from climbing up. Soon his arms ached with his heavyweight and became tired and numb, and despite all his efforts, they relaxed slowly, his struggling body slid down the pole. The rope gripped his neck. He twisted and strangled to a slow death in front of the mob. Gurgling sounds emitted from his mouth as his thick tongue hung out and his eyes bulged. Big Nose, George Parrott's life of killing slipped away mercilessly. His body released its fluids, and the stench of urine and feces assailed the mob's noses.

The men walked away, leaving the body to dangle, saying to each other, "Got what he deserved." Darn right, he did." Should have been hung sooner." Good riddance, I say.

(Note: George Parrott, also known as Big Nose, was hung by a lynch mob in Rawlins while Jim Averill was incarcerated there. George's partner, "Dutch"

Charlie Bates was lynched from a telegraph pole in "Hell On Wheels" coal mining town of Carbon County.

The local newspaper reported that no one who was part of the vigilante mob was charged with a crime. When the body came down, they found Big Nose had rubbed a large section of one ear off while he fought against the pressure of the rope around his neck.)

*   *   *

Dear sister Sarah and brother-in-law Able, and my little nephew Ralph,

I take pen in hand to bring you the latest news since my last writing. I wrote to you earlier that a grand jury was to be held on Charlie Johnson's death. The jury met and ruled to dismiss the murder charges as I was in the military, and therefore, the army should decide the case.

I rode back to Fort Fred Steele. The military did not pursue the murder charges in a civilian town against a civilian, but I was absent without leave, so I was demoted to private and fined $50.00. I requested to be assigned to Fort McKinney. The army denied the request, as I was almost through with my second enlistment, so they assigned me to work in the quartermaster's job until June 19, 1881 when I will be discharged with honor. I will come home. I do not plan on reenlisting.

Looking forward to seeing you all again.

Jimmy.

JAMES AND SOPHIA

CHAPTER SIX

Jim picked up the wood he had chopped and filled the wood box on the outside of the kitchen wall. He made sure the kindling went in, so the bottom pieces were against the leather covering the opening into the kitchen. Satisfied, his sister could stay in the warm kitchen and reach down to the hole in the wall, lift the leather covering and pull out the wood she would need for the stove, he walked into the kitchen.

"Jim, you've been home two entire months and have not said a word about what you would like to do," said Sarah.

Jim took off the flannel shirt he wore over his old army shirt. "I want my own place in the Wyoming Territory. I scouted around and found many places to make a home."

"Sounds wonderful. I'm glad you're settling down. I worried about you being in the army. When do you think you want to head back to the Wyoming Territory? In the Spring, I imagine." Sarah took the black stove lid pry bar and lifted the round cover of the stove and put in a piece of wood to feed the fire. She put the lid back on and hung the pry bar on a hook.

"Yep. I'd like to be near Rawlins in May. But first, I want to marry."

"Marry?" Sarah shifted and faced her brother with teeth showing in her smile. "Are you thinking of Sophia Jaeger?"

"I sure am. How did you figure it out?"

"Every Sunday after church, you catch up with her family and walk with them. When we're in town, and you see her, you smile and make an excuse to talk with her. Do you think she wants to marry you and move to the Territory?"

"I already asked her, and she said yes. But now I need to ask her father and get his blessing."

"Whooo-ee. When will you face that challenge?"

"Tonight. I'm going to take a bath, shave, put on by best clothes, and go to her house after supper."

"Oh, Jim. I hope everything goes well. Mr. Jaeger is a strict man. He came from Prussia and hasn't let go of the Prussian culture."

"Wish me luck." Jim got down the huge, galvanized washtub from the back entry. He put it in the kitchen. Later, he would heat water for the bath.

"Good luck."

*   *   *

"Come in, Jim," said Sophia as Jim entered the front door and took off his hat. "Poppa, Mr. Averell wants to talk to you."

Mr. Jaeger, while sitting in the parlor chair, filled his pipe. "About what?"

"Sir, I want to ask you for your daughter's hand in marriage."

"What?" Mr. Jaeger dropped his pipe in his lap, spilling tobacco.

"Sophia and I want to marry. We plan on going to the Wyoming Territory and homestead a ranch. The land is fertile, and I saved my army pay. We'll be happy there." Jim kept turning his hat in his hands as he stood before Mr. Jaeger.

"No! Absolutely not."

"Why, Poppa? Why?" asked Sophia. Tears flooded into her eyes.

"You are an educated, well-bred lady. He hasn't finished high school."

"I haven't, but I...."

"He is ten years older than you."

"Just nine, Poppa."

"Nine years. It doesn't matter. He is too old for you. And he wants to take you out to that savage and lawless country."

"Sir, it's safe I served there for years. The Indians aren't giving any trouble to the settlers. Besides, the army fort nearby handles all the renegade whites and Indians. The territory is safe for homesteaders. A hundred and sixty acres of land is free for each settler who wants to improve it. I've talked it over with Sophia, and she wants to do this." Jim's hat stopped twirling as he clenched it.

"Nein. No, I say again, no. You are not to marry this man." Mr. Jaeger stood.

Sophia took Jim's arm. "Poppa, I'm going to marry him. I want your blessing, but if you do not give it, I will marry him anyway."

"If you marry him. I will disown you. You'll never be welcomed in this house again."

Sophia's mother entered the parlor. "I heard everything from the kitchen. Johann, you can not mean that. She is our daughter."

"Stay out of this, Maria. You have no say. This is for the Poppa. Sophia, if you persist with this idea, you are to leave this house forever unless you return home in a box. Think about what I have said tonight. Decide tomorrow."

"I decide now. I'm going to marry Jim Averell. Jim, please wait for me outside. I'll go pack my things. I can stay with my brother Edward and his family until we are married." Sophia faced her parents. "You'll both be welcome at the ceremony if you wish to attend." Sophia spun from her father and mother with a straight back as she walked to her room.

Jim went out to the porch. Maria sobbed as she collapsed on a chair. Johann Jaeger stormed into the kitchen, yelling.

* * *

"Sophia, you made a beautiful wedding dress to wear today. You're a lovely bride. Jim is one lucky fella. Are you ready?"

"Yes, dear Edward," said Sophia, as she took her brother's arm. "I want to thank you and your family for letting me live here and hold my wedding here. It's so wonderful to have all my brothers and sisters and their families here today. And dear mama came. That took courage."

The two strode toward the parlor, crammed with people. "We couldn't miss this festive day, your wedding and to top it off, it is your twenty-second birthday. February 23, 1882, will be a day for two celebrations from now on." Edward smiled as the two approached Reverend Robert Blackburn.

Edward stepped back, and Jim stepped forward. Smiling, his head bent slightly, he gazed at his bride and took her hand.

Snowflakes swirled around the window panes which Jack Frost brushed during the night. In the magical and hushed world, Jim and Sophia said their vows.

*   *   *

With shaking hands, Sophia opened the letter from Sand Creek, Wyoming Territories. A thin piece of paper fell to the floor as she opened the sheet of paper. She picked up the dropped item and saw it was a railroad ticket to Rawlins. Her face lit up. Hurriedly reading the letter, she ran out the back of her brother's house to the yard. "Edward! Edward, Jim sent for me. He enclosed a ticket to Rawlins. He filed a 160-acre claim at a place called Sand Creek and started building our house. It isn't finished yet, but he wants me to come and stay with some friends of his, the Cantlin family. As soon as the house is finished, we can move in. As he took the furniture with him when he left here, it will be furnished when we move in. Won't that be wonderful?" Sophia twirled around while holding the letter and ticket in her hands up to the sky.

"Great, sister. Do you know when to leave?"

"Right away. He wants me there in early May, and it is already mid-April. I'll be with him when our baby is born. Whooo-eee."

*　*　*

My dear brother and sister -in-law,

Jim met me at the train station in Rawlins. It was raining, so we stayed in Rawlins for two days until the soggy roads dried up.

On May 7th, we hired a buggy and drove fifty-five miles to a tiny hamlet called Sand Creek. Jim says it's in the Sweetwater Valley. It's much nicer than Rawlins.

As Jim had not yet finish our home, he arranged for me to stay with the Cantlin Family. They took me in and treat me like one of their own. I've a comfortable bed with a mattress, windows to let in the cheery sunlight and a colorful woven rag rug on the puncheon floor. I'm so thrilled.

Jim had my beautiful Prussian-made, brass-pendulum wall clock in black walnut with frosted-glass swans shipped here and placed in our home. I'm eager to see it.

My deepest regards,

Sophia Averell

*　*　*

August 28, 1882,

Dear Sister Sarah and brother-in-law, Able,

Sophia wrote to her family and you that she stayed with loyal friends, the Cantlins, while I worked on our house and did work for others to earn money. She became like one of their own family.

My dear Phila (Sophia's nickname) gave birth to our little boy three months early. He arrived on the 23rd inst. At 6:30 AM and stayed with us until 1PM that day. He cried from the time he was born until he put a little hand over each eye and died.

Phila is doing well, and we have rented a suitable house to live in Rawlins as soon as she can travel.

Love to your son Ralph, and you both,

Jimmy.

P.S. We have not written to anyone on the subject but you and Sophia's sister, but of course we will tell them in time.

Your loving brother and sister,

Sophia and James Averell.

*   *   *

Cora Cantlin worried about Sophia. She asked her sister-in-law, Jane, to come and help her care for Sophia.

Each day, Sophia ate less and less. Cora could not entice her to eat more than a few swallows. Cora, Jane, and Jim feared she had "childbed fever."

"Jim, you need to go to Rawlins and find a doctor as fast as you can." Cora dipped a cloth in a basin of cool water, wrung it out, and put it on Sophia's burning forehead.

"I'll leave right now. It's about a ninety-mile round trip. I'll go as fast as I can. Please keep her alive until the doctor gets here and helps her." Jim did not wait for an answer. He grabbed his hat, saddled his horse and galloped out of the corral.

*   *   *

Dr. Thomas Maghee examined Sophia. He straightened up from his bent position over her bed. Turning to face Jim, Cora, and Jane, he said, "I'm sorry, there is little time left for her. There is nothing I can do." He closed his bag and walked out the bedroom door.

Jim stared at Sophia's chalk-white thin face. His body trembled as he swallowed hard. He took his wife's hand and knelt beside the bed. "My dear Sophia, my Philia, please don't leave me. Please.

Jim wrote to Sophia's mother, Marie.

*   *   *

September 6, 1882

My dear mother, and all who love my beloved wife,

Phila lost our baby by miscarriage on the23rd inst., and I'm heartbroken to say, but the chances are against her living much longer. It's sad news for you, and I'm heartbroken and loathe to tell you. O, my only beloved one on earth. I know I will follow her soon.

Your loving son,

James Averell.

*   *   *

Jim stayed by his wife's bed day and night. Sophia, often awake and aware, would talk with him about little things. She asked questions about his boyhood, and she told him about her childhood.

Each day became a little harder and less talk. Sophia slept more and more. One day she woke from her nap and smiled at Jim, who was holding her hand as he sat on the edge of her bed. "Jimmy, please tell everyone that I love them all. Please be sure you do that."

I will my dear. I will." Jim's voice choked, and he blinked away tears as he smiled at her.

Sophia gazed at him with smiling eyes before she closed them. Within a few moments, her breathing stopped.

Jim slid off the bed and dropped to his knees as he convulsed in sobs.

*   *   *

Jim took Sophia's body and the baby's by train to Sophia's family in Eureka, Wisconsin. The family placed the coffin in the parlor of her parents' home.

Trees were in a glorious fall bloom of golden, red and yellow leaves. The grass, still green in places, shimmered in the bright sunlight. A cool breeze rustled the leaves, making paper whispery music. A male Cardinal was chittering for his mate and Black-capped chickadees trilled in the trees.

Before the service, Johann Jaeger stared at Sophia's body and said, "She looks nice. Now close the coffin."

"Poppa, mother will want to see her," said Edward.

"Nein. I forbid her to view Sophia. I forbid. Nail down the lid."

The brothers did as they were told. They carried the box to the cemetery.

A Second Day Advent minister, Mr. Sedgwick, from the nearby town Partage, Wisconsin, conducted the graveside funeral service. Jim's and Sophia's brothers and sisters and their families, Johann Jaeger, and his wife, Maria, huddled around the grave. After the brief service, each person shook hands except Mr. Jaeger, who refused to shake hands with Jim. The family departed for their homes. Nobody saw the beauty of the day.

Once inside their home, Marie took off her coat and hat. She sat in the kitchen. "You said Johann, she was not to return home unless it was in a box. Well, she came home in a box with your grandchild. How could you say that to our daughter:" Maria slumped in the chair and placed her elbows on the table. Tears flowed from her eyes and sobs erupted as she held her head and rocked back and forth.

Johann went behind the horse barn, where no one could see him as he paced and grieved.

Jim bought a single, one-way train ticket to Rawlins, Wyoming Territory.

*   *   *

Jim stepped off the train and rented a horse. Arriving at his log cabin, he stabled the horse and walked to the front door of the house that had not become a home. Entering, he listened to the silence. Sophia's hand-carved clock he had brought with him from Wisconsin stood silently in the corner. The pendulum had stopped. *I can never live here.*

After turning and walking out the front door, he locked it. Jim never stepped on the property again. He sold the land, buildings and furnishings, including Sophia's black walnut clock to brothers, Robert and Frederick Butler.

(Note: I copied the letters written by Sophia and Jim Averell with a few minor changes to clarify information for the reader.)

CHAPTER SEVEN

"Hi brother. How is married life?" George Bothwell shook hands with Albert.

"It's great. Margaretta and her two children have settled in our home in Los Angeles. She stands out in society as a well-bred, educated woman and her children are wonderful kids. The kids love the ranch in Sweetwater. They enjoy romping with the four wolf cubs I have there. Margaretta is not found of the ranch life. She prefers our winter home in Los Angeles and our place in Cheyenne. She enjoys wearing fancy clothes, floppy hats and high heel shoes, which are not the attire for the ranch."

Al led the way into the library. "Our brother, John, arrived yesterday, and we're discussing the investment opportunities."

George and Albert entered the library, and John stood and greeted his brother George. The three men sat on stylish chairs.

"Wow, Albert. The shelves are crammed full of books. If you get any more, you will need another room."

"Yes, most of the books are on geology and evolution. My favorite authors are Spencer, Huxley, Darwin, and Tyndall. They really know their stuff." Al waved his hand at the walls lined with filled bookcases. "Last year, Hiram M. Chittenden, I'm sure you have heard of him, visited me at my Sweetwater ranch."

"Haven't heard of him," said George.

"He's a famous naturalist, conservationist, and author. You must have."

"Nope." George smiled and looked at John who was also smiling while looking at the floor. *Albert has always liked showing off how smart he is, and he knows all the important people. He sure hasn't changed.*

Albert's eyebrows waggled in surprise before he said, "Well, let's talk business." Albert offered his brothers cigars. "George, I'm glad you could leave your pastoral duties in New York to come and get on the ground floor of my enterprise. A crew is drilling for oil in Utah as we speak. I hope to hear we have a gusher soon." Al poured brandy into three glasses on the table.

"Albert, are there other investors besides the three of us?" asked John.

After taking a swallow of brandy, Albert smoothed his mustache. "A few. Drilling for oil is expensive. That's why I thought others should come into this to share the cost before we discover the oil."

Al repositioned himself on the chair. "I wanted to invite you into another fantastic opportunity I have." Albert leaned forward. "You know I started a cattle ranch in Colorado, but I sold out as the newcomer grangers, the nesters, were moving in and fencing small acreage for farms. Can't make any money cattle ranching without open range for grazing. So, I started a new ranch in Wyoming Territory. Plenty of open range and access to water. I'm starting the Wyoming Land Improvement Company. Besides the 560 acres I bought for the ranch hub, I aim to buy more land to sell to the investors in the company for a town to be built. The town will have everything that is in other towns, such as a blacksmith shop, a newspaper, stores, and residential homes. I'm calling it The Town of Bothwell, and I figure it will be the capital when Wyoming becomes a state. With a town named Bothwell, you know I will be a driving force for its success and the name will draw investors. We all went to school back east and, with your degree from the Yale Divinity School, George, and mine as a civil engineer, it will encourage investors. What do you guys say? The company will sell shares in an irrigation project in Bear Lake, which is between Utah and Idaho. Another irrigation project I'm planning for the Sweetwater Valley and also a gold mine I'm looking into."

"Albert, I'm invested heavily in the oil well, and what you're saying is huge and would take a lot of money," said George.

"I'm tapped out with the oil well investment," said John. "How long do you think it will be before we could get a return on the oil investment?" John swirled the brandy in his glass.

"The oil well should come in any day now. You could get a loan and invest in the land development and pay back the loan when the well comes in. Any day, now.

George interrupted, "When it comes in, I can consider investing in the land deal."

"Certainly, it will. All the signs are good. The land investment in the irrigation project and the town would take longer to get the word out. We could take out ads in the eastern newspapers and print up flyers, but when the money people see the opportunity, I know they will jump in," said Albert. You two might not get in. As your brother I don't want you to miss this opportunity."

"I'll consider it," said John.

*   *   *

The Casper Weekly Mail newspaper carried the following story: On August 16, 1889, 'the Sweetwater Land and Improvement Company, which proposes to deal with land and water rights in the Sweetwater Valley, has been incorporated with a capital of $3000.00. The incorporators are John R. Bothwell, John C. Baird, J. C. Davis, E.P. Schoonmaker and Albert J. Bothwell'.

*   *   *

A few months later, Albert met with his brothers and other investors.

"Gentlemen, I' m glad you all could make it to the meeting. Unfortunately, I have bad news. The oil well is dry. No oil. Our investment is a bust. But of course, everyone knows an investment does not come with a guarantee."

"Albert, you said it was sure thing. I invested all my savings. I'll have to start over," said John.

"John, there are no guarantees. All investments have risks. The amount you invested is up to you."

John's forehead puckered, and George bit his lower lip. They both stood and left the room. The other investors followed them out the door. George left Los Angeles and never visited his brother, Albert, again.

*   *   *

Packed suitcases stood by the door of the Bothwell's home in Los Angeles. Margarette shepherd her two children out the door to a carriage waiting for her.

"Margaretta, you are overreacting. Yes, the twin girls are mine with the ranch housekeeper, Alice Wadsworth. But they live at the ranch and will not be an issue in the social circles here in Los Angeles. If you would go to the ranch with me, I wouldn't have taken up with the housekeeper."

"Not an issue? Do you think I will stay here when you have a mistress and children by her? You show a photograph of the twins to all you want to impress. You like to boast about having twins, as if it were a great accomplishment. We're through." Margarette gave her husband a dirty look as she pulled a white glove on her hand. The two children, in the carriage by this time, slumped back in the seat. Their mother, with a stiff, straight back stepped into an ornate carriage and the driver closed the door and mounted the vehicle's seat.

Albert stood in the open door, staring at the disappearing vehicle pulled by two groomed geldings with sparkling harness.

CHAPTER EIGHT

Swarms of prospectors covered the Black Hill. Each man hoped to find the mother lode of gold and chop out a mine from the hills to land them in luxury.

The town of Deadwood grew at a fantastic rate. Miners needed supplies, food, clothing, blankets, lanterns, and mining equipment. An assayer's office helped the lucky ones brought in gold and walked out with money. Stores sprung up at a fast pace, but even faster, the saloons and brothels appeared.

A man in a suit stood out amongst the grubby prospectors as he dismounted and walked around the piles of rock and dirt to a man standing near a mine entrance, he asked, "Do you own this mine?"

"Sure do. It's called the Golden Terra. Why?"

"My name is John Henry Durbin. I own some butcher shops and slaughterhouses in Cheyenne and supply meat to the military forts in Wyoming. I came to Deadwood to branch out. I'm not interested in prospecting and digging for gold myself. I want to buy an existing mine, like yours. If you're interested, I think we can come to an agreement."

"I sure am. I've made plenty from the mine and want to move to California. I figured if I didn't stay here, someone would claim jump my holdings. Selling out would be the answer."

"Good," said John Durbin. "I aim to stay and open a gold-stamp mill and a bank."

"Let's talk money." The mine owner and John walked to a crude building near the entrance of the Golden Tera.

* * *

The Deadwood sheriff strode into the bank. "Mr. Durbin, I need to talk with you."

"Come into my office, sheriff. What's on your mind?" "You're shipping some gold out tomorrow, right?" "Yes, by stage."

"I think there will be trouble. I've heard from a friend that there might be some fellas intending to rob it. We need to stop it before it happens."

"That's serious." John Durbin sat at his desk, folded his hands, and rubbed his thumbs together as he thought. "Most of the gold is from my Golden Terra mine and my gold stamp-mill."

"When do you plan to make a shipment?" asked the sheriff.

"Tomorrow. It's going out on the regular stage."

"How do you want to handle it? Maybe you can ship the gold next week?"

"No. It needs to go out tomorrow." John Durbin gazed at the customers in the bank. He blew out his breath in a slight whistle. Tom Sun owns two gold mines and I have one and we're shipping out gold. It's headed for Cheyenne. Let's plan to get it through."

* * *

The sun poured its heat on the backs of the four horses hitched to the stage. The stagecoach driver slapped the reins and shouted to the horses as they pounded up the steep dirt road between the cliffs.

The passengers in the coach coughed as the dust entered the windows. The men fanned their faces with their haps and the women held their linen handkerchiefs over their mouths to block the dirt from their noses and mouths.

"What's that?" a woman yelled.

"A gunshot!" said a male passenger.

Four men on horses dashed out from behind boulders. "Stop!"

The driver jammed hard on the brake beam and pulled hard on the reins. The horses cried in pain as the bits tore into their mouths.

One rider aimed his rifle at the driver just as the coach came to a jerking stop, throwing the passengers about. The bandit pulled the trigger, and the driver slumped into the driver's box. Blood seeped onto his vest. Another man climbed onto the coach's roof.

"Everyone out." Robbers yelled at the passengers.

The four passengers got out. The women dropped their string purses while the men tossed their leather wallets onto the ground.

"It ain't here. There's no gold," said the thief on the roof.

"Let's get what the passengers have. We don't want to leave empty-handed."

While the robbers dismounted and gathered up the loot, a terrified passenger yelled, "Run!"

The women lifted their skirts and followed the men's example and scattered into the roadside boulders.

"This could be a trap. Let's get out of here. A posse may be close by."

The horses, frighted by the noise and confusion, jostled each other. The man on the stagecoach jumped down and mounted his skittish bronc. All the outlaws galloped up the road leading out of Deadwood.

The passengers came out of hiding and huddled together near the dead coachman.

"What do we do? It's too far to walk back to town, and we shouldn't go forward. We might come across the outlaws. What should we do?" said the passengers.

As they milled about, they heard the hooves and shouts coming from Deadwood. They recognized a second coach bearing down on them. They stood at the roadside. Waving and shouting, they stopped the coach. It had a driver, the sheriff, and two armed guards. Amid cries of relief, the passengers entered the coach, which carried gold bullion.

The sheriff stepped off the coach and examined the dead driver. "Well, Mr. Durbin kept his gold."

One guard put the body into the back boot of the coach.

Picking up the reins of the first coach, he brought up the rear.

* * *

"Durbin, I just got the word the bullion got through. Your plan worked. Only the first coach driver was killed. He had a wife and three kids," said the deputy sheriff as he entered the bank's office.

Durbin sighed relief. "Thanks for letting me know. I was worried. It's hard to sit here and not be in control."

"It's likely we won't get the bandits, though. They scattered and there are plenty of places to hide in the Black Hills."

John Durbin lit a cigar as he smiled. "That's okay. We got the gold out. Too bad about the driver, but he knew it could happen."

"Yeah." The deputy stared at Durbin. "Guess so. Too bad he leaves a wife and kids behind." The deputy left the office, shaking his head.

*   *   *

The family carriage pulled up to the front door of Durbin's new Cheyenne house. John stepped out and reached back to help his wife Emma and their two daughters. A second carriage had their four sons. The driver helped unload the boxes, hatboxes, and bags. He put them on the walk in front of their posh home.

Emma and the girls entered the house, followed by John and the coachman with some luggage.

A servant came forward.

"Girls, go with the maid to your rooms. Your father will bring up your things later." Emma turned to her husband. "John, it's so wonderful to move to Cheyenne. Finally, we are back in civilization."

"Yes, dear, here we will stay. I sold my gold mine, but I kept the stamp mill. I'm tired of banking. Too sedentary. I want to move about, not go to the same place each day for work. After dinner, we can talk about our future. I've more plans."

*   *   *

After a dinner of Wild Apple Maple Duck, scalloped tomatoes, and Quick Fruit upside-Down Gingerbread, John and Emma went into the parlor.

"John, are you going back into the slaughterhouse business? It's lucrative, but it isn't a status."

"No, dear, my brother can continue to handle that side of my business. I'm going into cattle ranching and joining the Wyoming Stock Growers Association. I've hired a man named Collins as the foreman. It will be the UT near Split Rock. I'm also in contact with two brothers, Nate and Clabe Young. Clabe is the foreman for Tom Sun's ranch. Tom is a good man, and he started his ranch with the gold he got from his mines. Clabe and Nate are savvy men who know how to get the herd size to grow. My dear, we have millions now, but the ranch will bring us millions more. You wait and see."

Emma hugged her husband. "Is your Irish heritage the cause of your Midas touch or your ambition?" She smiled as she released her husband from the hug.

They both laughed. "It's both, my dear, both.

*   *   *

"Hey John," said Thomas Durbin. John's brother entered the butcher shop's main room from the back room, where enormous slabs of beef were stacked. He wiped his bloody hands on a thick cloth apron. "this idea of yours of buying Amos Peacock's two butcher shops was great. Are you glad you got out of the banking business, in Dakota?"

"Am I ever. The banker's life is not for me. When William Randolph Hearst offered to buy my Golden Terra mine, it was the perfect solution." John watched his brother sharpen his butcher cleaver. "Yeah. My cattle ranch with hundreds of beefs on the open range, we'll have a good supply of meat for Cheyenne, the military forts and even ship back east. John brushed away flies gathering over the meat and blood. "I made friends with Nate and Clabe Young. Rumor is they are cattle rustlers. They're going to increase my herd and I'll see to it they get a hefty denaro."

"How does Emma like living in that new home you built here in Cheyenne?"

"Great. She is a wonderful mother to our four sons, and she treats her two stepdaughters just as if they were hers. She deserves a modern house in the best neighborhood of Cheyenne and the society of my membership in the Wyoming Stock Growers Association. I aim to be the richest man in the West. No one is going to stop me."

I'm happy for you, John Henry." Tom selected a slab of beef and hefted it onto the butcher table.

CHAPTER NINE

A mustache covered his upper lip and merged with his beard, which extended past the top of his necktie. The color of the tie blended with the somber suit. The boiled stiff shirt collar visible under the tie and suit coat made a slight red line on his neck where it chafed. The man extended his hand to the cowhand, who walked up the front steps of the Cheyenne home.

"Mr. Hayworth, I take it. You were recommended to me as a dependable man to be the foreman of my ranch, the T Bar T."

"Yes, sir, Mr. Galbraith. I can do the job. I understand your ranch is thirty miles from Rawlins."

"Yes, but I plan to expand it to the Sweetwater Valley. The open grazing land is plentiful, so there is room for much larger herds. However, you will need to hire more men than what is at the ranch now."

The two men sat on wicker rockers on the porch.

"I'm sure you know the government is cracking down on the free grazing land and is dividing the land into 160-acre homesteads. That will chop up the land into small farms. There will be no grazing land for the large herds in a few years," said Mr. Hayworth.

Robert Galbraith ran his finger through his beard as he stared at the horse and buggy traffic. "I've had hard work all my life. I've been in charge of railroad yards in Omaha, then Cheyenne until the Central Pacific and Union Pacific linked up in Utah. Later, I was in charge of the yards at Laramie, at the coal mines of Benton. Benton was connected to the railroad yard at a tent town called 'Hell on Wheels'. Which it was aptly named. There were over a thousand men in the tent town on weekends. Gunfights, fist fights, skull cracking, hangings and murder. Finally, I had all I could stand and left." Galbraith shifted in his chair and sent it rocking. "I married Ophelia. Now, I'm leaving that rotten life behind. I have enough money to make my cattle ranch into an empire. "He shifted his gaze back to Hayworth. "I'm used to a fight, whether it is men or the government. The Federal Government doesn't understand what life is like out here and the problems encountered with raising beef to put on their plates. There are ways to get around their lack of foresight, however. Each man you hire, including yourself, will need to make a 160-acre claiming it in his name, his parents, sister's, brother's, and cousin's names. Even the dead could make claims. Put all the claims together and that will provide the grazing land. I'll pay each man fifty cents an acre he claims under any name he uses. After the claim is established, I'll buy it from him. All the big cattle men are doing it."

"The men will love that."

"Get started right away. My family and I'll spend the summers at the ranch and the winters here in Cheyenne. However, I ran and won a seat in the Territorial Legislature for Carbon County, so I won't be at the ranch for a month while the legislature is in session. Do you think you can handle things?"

Hayworth stood, extended his hand, as he said, "I sure can. You can trust me."

Robert Galbraith stood, and after shaking hands, the two men separated. He put on his bowler hat and strolled to meet Tom Sun and Albert Bothwell at the Cheyenne Cattlemen's Club.

* * *

"Hey, there, Robert Galbraith, wait up."

Robert turned as he stepped out the door of the Wyoming Territorial House of Representative.

A gust of wind swept up the street. He grabbed his hat as it shot forward. Replacing his Bowler, he smiled at a fellow representative.

"The Wyoming Stock Growers Association should give you a medal for your efforts in passing the Maverick Law. Now the unbranded calves found on the open range are to be branded with an M on the neck and they become the calves owned by the Association to be auctioned off to the highest bidders who are appointed by representatives of the association with a registered brand from the state. Great Work." The man slapped Galbraith on the back.

Robert shook hands with the fellow member, Bob Conner.

Bob Connor continued, "It will keep the nesters and small ranchers from expanding. It will help us big cattle men a lot. You maneuvered the bill through the house expertly. The small ranchers are out of luck."

"Even if the small outfits get a registered brand, they won't be able to outbid the big stockmen at the auction. It'll keep the little guys out and lets the big ranchers add to their herds. And it's all legal." Galbraith smiled, showing his yellow teeth. "Glad the session is over for the year, though. I want to get back home to Cheyenne," said Galbraith.

"Me, too. Likely see you in Cheyenne," said Conner, as he tipped his hat.

Galbraith grinned as he walked to his carriage to begin his trip home.

CHAPTER TEN

"Oh, ladies, isn't this glorious? Nothing finer can be found back East, I'm sure. We can sit on this spacious veranda and view the beautiful lawns and grounds on three sides of the building. Won't that be lovely on hot summer days?" Mrs. Mary Agnes Sun asked.

The women walked into the dining room. "Oh, my! Red velvet drapes from the ceiling to the floor and such thick carpet. Notice there are dumb waiters to bring food from the basement kitchen to the dining room. " said Mrs. Ophelia Galbraith. "What luxury.

"The mirrors! They are diamond-shaped and so tall. They perfectly reflect the potted palm trees and overstuffed velour upholstery of the chairs. Such elegance." Mary Agnes Sun brushed hand white gloved hand over the back of a chair.

"Look at these rooms. The men have this billiard room, a card room, and a reading lounge with tooled leather furniture, said Mrs. McLean.

"A perfect place for the ball after the opening night of the Opera House's premiere season," said Mary Agnes.

"Is anyone aware what the dinner menu will be?" asked Emma Durbin.

"Yes, I talked to the chef. The appetizers will be pickled eel, black or green stuffed olives and fresh oysters on the half shell." Ophelia kept her smile on her face as if announcing ice cream sundaes.

Several women glanced sideways at the others, trying not to let the smiles fade from their faces.

"Following will be Blue Winged Duck with Richelieu Ragout and Larded Tendons of Veal a la Jacquemiere. The desserts will be Whipped Syllabub and Peach Meringue a la Francis."

Genuine smiles returned to everyone's face as they continued to tour the club.

"Ladies, aren't we fortunate to be married to such wonderful and considerate husbands? The Cheyenne Club is for the men, but they are so gracious to allow balls and parties which we can attend in such a lavish and splendid facility."

All the ladies nodded in agreement.

*   *   *

"Let's let our wives enjoy the room, gentlemen, while we go to the smoking lounge and have our cigars," Galbraith said.

Several cattlemen followed Galbraith into a rich mahogany wood paneled room, which contained a fireplace with over-stuffed comfortable chairs. The men picked their preferred seats and lit their Havana cigars.

"Did anyone like the opera?" asked Tom Sun.

The men rolled their eyes and made faces to show their answer.

"I know the wives enjoyed it," said John Durbin.

"How so, John?" asked Albert Bothwell.

"It gave them the excuse to have those large hairdos with flouncy feathers on top and those jeweled brocaded evening gowns with trains. They like all that doll-up stuff and the more expensive, the better. My wife's dress cost twenty-five dollars."

The men laughed.

"Hey, Tom, your wife told mine you served in the army with the famous Buffalo Bill Cody." Galbraith held the match to his cigar as he puffed several times to get it started.

"Yeah, we both were army scouts and guides at Fort Fred Henry. Buffalo Bill recently sent me one of his rifles he used in his Wild West show."

"Wow. What a keeper," said Albert Bothwell. "But seriously, I understand the Wyoming Cattlemen's Association told you, you would need to leave the Association, because you employ Clabe Young, a known cattle thief, as your foreman."

Shifting in his chair, Tom replied, "Yes, but that's been straightened out. I fired Clabe and hired his brother Nate." To change the topic, Tom puffed on his cigar before he said, "Galbraith, I heard you guided some scientist to Separation Rock to observe the solar eclipse. Bet that was interesting."

"Yes. They were decent enough fellows, but somewhat peculiar. One man, Thomas Edison, wanted me to take him fishing after the eclipse. We went up into the Sierra Madre Mountains. We found a fishing spot on Battle Lake. Edison had a bamboo fishing rod, which he broke while fishing. Later, he threw it into the fire at our camp site. He sat on a rock and stared at it for the longest time. I asked him why he kept looking at it. He said he was amazed at how long it took the fibers to burn. First, they glowed without disintegrating. He thought that was unusual. He kept staring and staring at the rod. I thought that was an odd thing to be interested in, how something burns. Scientists are strange."

Tapping his cigar ash into a tray, Albert Bothwell faced Tom. "How are your gold mines in the Seminoe Mountains doing, Tom?"

Squaring his shoulders and holding his head high, he said, "The Desert Treasure and Emeletta are doing well." Tom smiled as he inhaled and blew out a smoke ring.

"Emeletta? That is an odd name," said Conner.

"Named after my first girlfriend."

The men laughed.

"Does your wife know?"

"Hope not."

The men chuckled.

Throat clearing by Bothwell grabbed everyone's attention. "You are building waterwheels on the Sweetwater river and Cherry Creek. Why, Tom?"

"Cattlemen need to take care of the range. It's being overgrazed. All cattle owners are part of the problem. I want to raise the water high enough to irrigate the higher lands. I'm afraid it is too little and too late, but an effort needs to be made. We need to think about what we will leave to our children."

Bothwell spoke up, "Those nesters are the big problem. The Desert Land Act the government passed allows any fool to homestead 160 acres any place he wants on public land. The only condition is he must improve it in five years or three years if he was in the military. This gives the nesters the idea they can fence off small sections to keep our cattle off what they say is their land. That means less grazing land for our stock, and it keeps them away from the water. We were here first. I say it's our land. We put up our barbed wire around our hayfields and grazing areas. We took on that expense and of raising and shipping the cattle back East to feed their constituents."

"Galbraith, that was a top-notch move on your part to back the Maverick Law in the legislature," said McLean.

"Yes, it made us able to get the unbranded calves born in the Spring into our herds and not the nesters,"

The men laughed and puffed on their cigars. Bothwell told a servant to bring more Martell brandy for the men.

An hour later, Joh Durbin asked, "Do you think our hens are ready to go home?"

Glancing at his pocket watch, McLean said, "Reckon not. Only one o'clock in the morning. Guess they'll be clucking away for a least another hour."

All the cocky men guffaw.

CHAPTER ELEVEN

Throwing himself into work eased Jim's grief over the loss of his baby and wife, Sophia. He started another homestead fifteen miles from the first, and in July 1885, he filed the claim. The new homestead was between Horse Creek and Sweetwater River in Carbon County. After he built the log house off the main road, he constructed a log building to be a small store, a bar, and a restaurant next to the road.

"Nephew, I'm sure glad you came to visit for a spell. I need to go to Rawlins to buy supplies. I'll be back tomorrow. Can you watch after the road ranch?"

"Sure can, Uncle Jim," said Ralph Cole. When ma and pa said I should come out to Wyoming and visit with you, they were right I'm glad I did."

"Glad you did too. Thanks, Ralph." Jim slapped the reins and the horse moved forward, pulling the buckboard.

Several hours later, as the sun shimmered on the horizon, he tied up at the hitching rail in front of the Mercantile. After paying for and loading the buckboard with flour, salt, sugar, coffee, oats, beans, tobacco, and nails, Jim covered everything with a canvas.

He drove the wagon over to the Rawlins House. The hotel had a restaurant, and the delicious fragrance of fresh bread, strong coffee, and beefsteak found its way out the door and to Jim's nose.

After he snaffled a weight on the horse's bridle, he stepped into the dining area and sat at a round table.

A woman with dark hair tied back from her face and wearing a plain apron over her dress stepped out from the kitchen. She delivered two meals to a couple seated at another table. She walked over to Jim.

"Yes, sir. Do you want a full meal or just coffee and bread?"

"What is the full meal?" asked Jim.

"A slab of seared beef, peeled and boiled potatoes, fresh butter, fresh-baked bread, and a cup of coffee. That's 15 cents. Just coffee and bread with butter are 5 cents."

"I'll take the full meal. Thank you."

"The fella that owns this hotel, he and his wife are celebrating their 15th anniversary. He said anyone who orders a full meal today gets a piece of Scripture Cake with Burnt Jeremiah Syrup for free, if 'en the customer wants it."

"I surely do. Ain't had any cake since I was knee high to a mare."

"Yes, sir. Right away."

The waitress later returned with a platter filled with food and a cup of coffee. The eating utensils she pulled from her pocket. "Here you are, Sir. That will be 15 cents."

Jim took out a leather pouch and paid her. "You're new to Rawlins, ain't you?"

"Yes. I moved here from Cheyenne. The city was too noisy and busy for a farm girl like me. Tell me if you ain't satisfied with somethin.'" She left and disappeared into the kitchen.

Jim cut the thick slice of meat. While chewing the beef, his eyes widened and blinked. *This beef isn't tough and it's flavorful. The potato was firm, and the bread was soft, but not mushy or crumbly.* After he enjoyed every mouthful, he thought, *This is sure better than army cooking, and I admit the food is better than Sophia's. Dear Sophia.* Blinking away tears forming in his eyes, he got up and walked to the kitchen door. He stepped into the hot room where the waitress was standing by the cook stove.

"I'd like to know who the pot rustler was."

"I am. Wasn't everything all right?"

"The victuals were right tasty. So, you made the bread and cooked the potatoes and the meat?"

"Yes."

"I've a homestead, and I'm opening a road ranch with a restaurant. A place for travelers and cowpunchers to stop and eat a hot meal. There are a couple of rooms to rent for overnight stays and a small bar, and some supplies people may run short of. If you would come and run the restaurant, you could charge twenty-five cents a meal and keep fifteen cents."

"I couldn't travel from town every day. Where would I live? And I have two boys I'm looking after. John DeCorey is only 14, and Gene Crowder is 11; I can't leave them behind."

"Bring them with. You could have a homestead right next to mine. You could build for the future. I could build your cabin to be a half-hour walk from mine. The land would be 160 acres you would own after five years. By the way, what's your name?"

"Ellen Watson. And yours?"

"James Averell. Folks call me Jim. Is it a deal?" Ellen wiped her hands on her apron and held it out to shake. "Yes."

Jim shook her hand. "Done. We've had a terrible drought this spring and summer. I know the best place for you to stake a claim. The Sweetwater Creek is running nearby. You could plant vegetables next Spring.

"It sounds like hard work, but we'll be up for it," said Ellen.

*   *   *

The horses pulled the wagon over the parched ground and stopped in front of a two-room cabin made of fir logs. Ellen and the two boys jumped down from their perches on their belongings and ran to the door. Jim snaffled a weight to the horse before he carried some bags into the cabin.

"Jim, this is great. A window on each side lets in the light, and they have flower boxes. There is a sturdy door painted a cheery green. The place has plenty of room for the boys and me to sleep with room for a small table and chairs and a heat stove."

"I figure you and the boys can eat at my place up the road as you're cooking meals, or you can bring food back here. In the winter, the heat stove is more important than the cookstove." Jim set down a wooden barrel and started for the door. "Next spring, you can plant vegetables and start putting in barbed wire fencing to keep roaming cattle off your land, and later you can buy some cattle and keep them on your property."

"This is wonderful, boys, ain't it?" Ellen gazed out the window at the prairie and trees in the distance. *Life is good. Now, the boys and I have a wonderful future*, Ellen thought. "Let's help bring in our things from the wagon, boys."

*   *   *

"Ellen, we have been working together for a few months, which isn't a lot of time, but I feel we are comfortable with each other fairly well. We each have filed our homesteads and are proving them up, and together, we're making an income to sustain us and a bit more. I was wondering if you would consider marriage?" Jim rearranged items on the shelf. "Out here, we do little courting and such things. We ain't got time, with the chores and all." From the collar of his shirt to his hairline, Jim's face flushed red.

"I told you I'm a divorced woman, and my former husband was a drunkard and beat me. Since the boys and I have been here, I have never seen you drink, and you seem to have a genteel manner. I think getting hitched would be the best thing for both of us and the boys. They like you. It's the sensible thing to do." Ellen finished putting the coffee grinder on the table. "When should we do it?"

A deep breath of relief escaped from his mouth as Jim said, "It's early in the morning. The sun isn't up for another hour. Let's go now to Lander on the Shoshone Indian Reservation. My Nephew Ralph can look after the boys. The trip is 105 miles each way. And we will need about six days to go, file, marry, and return. Is that okay with you?" Jim smiled and turned to face Ellen.

"Sure, but why so far?"

"If we marry in Rawlins, where people know us, we can't each claim 160 acres. So, we need to keep the marriage quiet until we have titles to the land."

"Let's go," said Ellen.

They packed a change of clothes, trail food, and water before they mounted their horses. After two days of riding over the prairie and sage brush with overnight camping, they rode into Lander.

On May 11, 1886, they signed the Application for a Marriage License and the Marriage License.

After two days in Lander, they rode for two days toward home.

*   *   *

"Ellen, we missed you." John and Gene jumped and hopped about as Ellen and Jim rode into the yard.

"I missed you, too. Were you good and did as you were told?"

"Ralph stood behind the boys. "They sure were. Helped with the chores, and they went to your place and checked on everything. They didn't even complain about my cooking."

"After I rest a day, I'll make us a special meal to celebrate. Can you boys take care of the horses for us?"

"Sure can." They said together.

FAMILY LIFE

CHAPTER TWELVE

Newspaper headline told the story. "Disaster Hits the Plains of Wyoming Territory!"

Blizzards hit the area in the winter of 1886-1887. The open range plunged into prolonged and disastrous weather of blizzards. Snow fell day after day in November. The snow would thaw and then freeze, piling itself higher and higher. Drifts filled the ravines and coulees until they were level. The granular flakes lay in enormous masses on the plateaus and river bottoms. The sun did not appear for weeks and weeks.

"Boys, the snow is not letting up, and the wind is piling it up in drifts. I'm going to tie this rope around my waist, and I want you to hold on to the other end, while I'll go out to the barn and attach the rope and follow it back. We'll tie this end to the door when I return, because, right now, I can see the barn, but a time may come when we can't and could get lost."

"I wish we were at Jimmy's ranch." Gene's lower lip trembled.

"Oh, I do too, honey, but no one can find out we are married. We each need to keep up our own places, so we don't lose one. We'll be fine."

"How about the privy, Ellen? Even in the cold, the chamber pot will become full and stinky.

"Top-notch thinking, John. I'll take a second rope to go from the house to the outhouse. We can use the chamber pot until we need to dump everything into the privy."

Ellen put on several layers of clothing. Her linen coat would not fasten because of the clothing under it. She tied a kerchief over her poke bonnet to hold it down and to cover her ears before tying the rope around her waist. She opened the door. It slammed back against her, hitting hard, as the wind caught it and blew it in with a bang. She pushed hard and made her way out, then she pulled the door shut as the two boys pushed on the other side and put in the bar.

The boys listened for her footsteps or her voice if she would call out. All they heard was the howl and shriek of the wind as it beat against the walls and shook the closed shutters. Their feet shuffled around the door as they waited nervously for Ellen.

"John, do you think we'll hear her at the door when she wants us to let her in?"

John tried to bore a hole through the door with his eyes.

Minutes dragged by. A half-hour went by. An hour, which seemed like two.

"Maybe we should open the door and see if she is out there," said Gene.

"Yeah."

As they lifted the bar, the door rattled in the frame. They heard Ellen pounding. The door flew open and hit the wall, bounced back, and flew open again. Ellen staggered in.

"Ellen, were you by the door long?" asked the boys together.

Ellen shook her head as she gasped for breath. When she could talk, she said, "I just got to the door, but I wouldn't have lasted long. That wind is biting cold and so strong it almost blew me off my feet. When I had to face it, snow and wind stung my eyeballs." Ellen sat by the woodstove and jerked spasmodically. "The snow is almost hip deep to the barn. I couldn't see my tracks from yesterday. I had to dig a path to the barn and dig the snow away from the door so I could get in to check on the animals. I should go out every day to keep the path open, maybe even twice a day. Boys, I think we are in for a long, long, hard, hard winter."

*   *   *

Snow and ice melted away under the warm sun and blue sky. The dead grass came to life and leaves were budding on the distant trees. The soil was soft and easy to plow.

"Now, ain't this a glorious day to be outside planting seeds? Everything is so green, and the fresh air in our lungs is invigorating. With the sod turned up real deep by the plow, we can now break up the clumps with the hoe."

"Ellen, why does the plow need to turn the earth? Can't we hoe up a hole, drop in a seed and make another hole?" Gene asked.

"My, my, no. The kernels need air as we do. By going deep into the soil and turning it over the air gets in."

"How come you know so much about seeds and stuff?" asked John.

"My pa and ma are farmers in Kansas."

"Well, I'm glad you came here and decided we could live with you. Why did you come to the Wyoming Territory?" asked John.

After a moment of silence, Ellen stopped hoeing and used the handle as a pole to lean on. The boys, kneeling in the dirt, continued breaking up small clumps.

A cardinal trilled in the distance. Chickens clucked and scratched in their fenced yard.

"Some memories aren't kind. I don't think about the past anymore. I was married once to William Pickell, who had a homestead next to my folk's place and he began courting me when I was sixteen."

"You were married before Jimmy?" asked John.

"Yes, I was. We got married on November 24, 1879. We had a lovely wedding at the farm and a photographer in town took our picture."

"Why aren't you married to him now? Did he die?" asked Gene.

"No, dear heart. He drank every day. He spent the nights with other women, and he beat me."

The boys stopped working and gaped at her. Their lower jaws dropped open. "He beat a woman?" both boys asked at once.

"Yes. The last time he used a horsewhip and kept hitting me until I was covered in red welts. I ran across the fields to pa's farm."

"What happened next?" asked Gene.

"Two years of marriage was enough. I divorced him and moved away. I finally moved to Cheyenne, where I got hold of you two rascals. And now we're here with our own place." Ellen reached down and tousled the boys' hair.

John fixed his gaze on the soil and began haphazardly to break up the clumps. "Did you take me in because my pa drinks?

"Partly, John. I noted your pa staggering around Cheyenne and figured you needed care after your ma died. Maybe, he was sad about losing your ma and started drinking. I'm sure he loves you, honey."

"He drank before ma died, only not so bad. We always had food. I was sad about ma, too, but now there wasn't enough food. I went hungry at night many times. That's why I helped to steal the pie from you."

"Did he beat you?" asked Gene.

"No, he drank until he staggered and fell. Slept where he landed." John sniffled as his fingers charged into the dirt. "Did your pa beat you, Gene?"

"Never knew my pa. Ma said he left before I was born. Ma worked at night and didn't want me hanging around, so…."

"So, when I spied John, taking my warm pie just out of the oven, I reckoned he was a bright young lad, and then I found you.

Gene and John, grinning, squinted at Ellen as she gave them a wink.

"The sun is shimming up the sky. We best get busy, or it will be harvest time, and we won't have our vegetables in."

The three laughed as they continued planting. Ellen said, "Boys, when we harvest these onions, we need to remember to look at them carefully."

"Why, Ellen?"

"Onions tell us the weather. If the onion's skin is very thin, mild winter's coming in: onion's skin is thick and rough, coming winter is cold and tough."

"We need a warning, for sure, if we're going to have another winter like the last one," said John.

They nodded in agreement and industriously applied their hoe and fingers.

WOE TO THE PROFESSIONAL THIEVES

CHAPTER THIRTEEN

"Howdy there, Mr. Durbin. I'm John Finkbone. Captain Turtle's Chicago Detective Agency appointed me to find and arrest Nate and Clabe Young and take them to Texas. They're wanted for murder and rustling. I heard you know most of the people in the area. Can you give me a lead on where I can find them?" John Finkbone shifted his weight in his saddle as he talked to John, who was standing on his ranch porch.

"Sorry, I've met the brothers, but I don't know where they are. Wish I could help you out." Mr. Durbin leaned against a porch post.

"All right, then. I'll mosey on to the other ranches in the Sweetwater area, to see if I can run into them." He reined his horse to back away from the porch and trotted off.

"Good luck." Mr. Durbin raised his hand and waved.

As soon as Mr. Finkbone was out of sight, Durbin went to the barn and saddled his horse. He rode to the Sweetwater valley and spotted Nate and Clabe on the prairie near the Sun ranch.

"Hey, Clabe and Nate, rein up. There's a detective looking for you to arrest and take to Texas. You should lie low for a while."

Nate and Clabe looked at each other. "Thanks, Mr. Durbin, for the warning. We'll be on the lookout." The brothers pressed their thighs against the saddles and the horses moved off at a walk.

*　*　*

"You're Clabe Young, aren't you?" The rider eased his bronc within a yard of Clabe's horse on the Sun's ranch grassland.

"Yeah." Clabe eyed the stranger, who had his hand near his holster. He put his horse on the bit to prepare for a fast run.

"I'm Finkbone and I'm arresting you for murder and horse rustling in Texas." With his horse on the bit and his posture straight with his butt deep in the saddle, he said, "Don't run for it You won't make it."

"It's a long way to Texas. Don't count on getting there," said Clabe.

*　*　*

On a blistering hot day, two dirty horses and riders pulled up at the hitching rail of a Texas jail. One rider dismounted, tied both horses to the rail, and pulled the other man, wearing handcuffs, off his horse. Shoved toward the jail's open door, the cuffed man staggered in, followed by his companion.

"Sheriff, I'm John Finkbone, hired by the Chicago Detective Agency to bring in Clabe Young for murder and rustling. Need a place to lock him up."

"Sure thing. He sure looks beat up," said the sheriff as he picked up the cell's keys and walked Clabe into the nearest cell.

Finkbone took the cuffs off the prisoner before walking to the office desk. "When a judge gets here, Young will confess to his crimes and then he can be sentenced."

"How do you know he's gonna' confess?"

After walking to the door, Finkbone said, "He will. I'm going to stable the horses. Be back later."

*   *   *

Days later, dust swirled in the air when a slight breeze entered through the jailhouse door. The air was stifling. The sheriff, judge and John Finkbone sat on chairs outside Clabe's cell.

"All right, you have confessed to your Texas crimes and now we want to hear what you were up to in Wyoming Territory. Afterwards, you will get a decent meal and a glass of beer," said the judge.

"You promise I won't hang?"

"No, just prison," said the judge.

Clabe's eyes darted from one man to another. "There is this big, important fella in England called Searight. He don't come to the States ever, but he owns maybe a million cattle on the open range. He got men working for him, but he never checks on them and so long as they get paid, they don't worry about losing some head.

The ranchers John Durbin and Bob Conner hired me and my brother to steal as many cattle as possible with the Searight brand. They figured Searight wouldn't ever know the cattle disappeared from the central and eastern sections of Wyoming. Last spring, we figure we took over a thousand head. He'll be lucky if he has any cattle left by next year. That Mr. Durbin blames the cattle rustling on the homesteaders, well, actually, all the big ranchers blame the nesters. And Mr. Conner has Lew Smith as his foreman, and he rustles as much as I did. But that Mr. Conner plays it smart, he does. He is a member of the Saint mark's Episcopal Church, so he looks like an upstanding guy.

"John Durbin and Bob Conner should be in jail with me as they stole the most cattle. They're responsible for my troubles. Go arrest them."

"I ain't been hired to go after those fellas. I'm gonna start looking for your brother, Nate. That's all I care about," said Finkbone.

"Sheriff, if this Englishman doesn't make any charges and doesn't even know his cattle are stolen there is no reason to go after Durbin and Conner," said the judge.

"Right."

The men left the jail, and the sheriff walked over to the saloon to get a glass of beer for Clabe.

CHAPTER FOURTEEN

"Hey, Averell, wait up. I want to talk with you."

Jim stopped in front of the harness shop in Rawlins. "Sure. What do you want, Bothwell?"

A bit of dust flew into the air as a dray wagon went by. A rider cantered by and collided with a rider on a mule and cursing filled the air.

"What do you mean writing that letter to the Casper Weekly Mail saying the Bothwell Town was 'A geographical expression' without a single building except for a shack?" Bothwell shoved his hat further back on his head. His loud voice added to the fray.

Jim stepped to the side of the door to let a customer leave. "Well, if the town exists, show me the stores, the blacksmith shop, and the post office your brochures tout. Where are they? The only building is a shack, and it's the Sweetwater Chief newspaper. You use the shanty to print your bogus pamphlets. This so-called investment town is one mile from Ella Watson's ranch. I should be able to see it, if 'en it was there." Jim smirked. "All you want is to sell land you own to unsuspecting folks out East for high prices. Folks don't have to buy your land to build and open a business. They have the Homestead Act."

"A town will be built. You have no business interfering in mine. I have a right to sell the land to investors if I want." Bothwell jabbed Jim's chest with his forefinger before stepping aside to allow two ladies to walk on the narrow boardwalk.

It's a fraud, simple as that. You say there is a town. There isn't. I'll let the people read the truth."

The ladies looked at the men when they heard their anger.

They kept walking.

"Small cattle ranchers are nesters. You fence in your small 160 acres so our cattle can't get to water. Nesters act so high and mighty, because you are given land by the government, and all you have is a pittance compared to us important ranchers. Stop causing trouble. Sell out. If you don't you will be sorry someday. You can't win."

"Is that a threat?" asked James.

"No, a promise," said Bothwell.

"Promise or threat. It doesn't matter. If the small ranchers took down the barbed wire and let their cattle out onto the free grazing land, all the calves born would become the property of the Wyoming Stockmen's Association, which sells the calves to the highest bidder. We fence. So our cattle stay on our land, and the calves are our land, and our brands go on them." James glared at Bothwell as he emphasized his words by pounding his finger on Bothwell's chest. "A full-grown steer is worth twenty dollars a head. I say, you keep your calves, and as you refer to us as nesters, will keep our calves." Jim gave a decided nod and went into the shop.

Albert followed Jim. "That cack-a-mammie idea of yours to divide the county into two pieces, one for the cattlemen and one for the nesters with their farms and small herds. It'll ruin the cattle industry, and you know it."

"Tain't right for three or four men to claim 75 miles of the Sweetwater River just for them. If the citizens divide the county in two sections, Wyoming can have orchards and farms producing potatoes, oats and food this country needs. Besides, I sold you a water easement on the Sweetwater River to irrigate your vast grazing land. That was a short time ago, May 14th, if I remember right. And you paid only thirty dollars, which seems fair to me, more than fair with all the trouble you cause me. Now, I got business to do."

"I shouldn't have to pay anything to cross your land for the water, and thirty dollars is a lot of money." Bothwell's face turned red.

Shaking his head, Jim said, "I ain't got time to talk with you." Jim walked over to the shelf of saddle soap.

Albert Bothwell set his jaw, turned, and walked away. *This isn't over. Not by a long shot.*

*   *   *

Later, Jim sat at the table and read through the newspaper while Ellen finished the kitchen clean-up.

"Hey, Ella, gander at this. The Casper Weekly Mail printed my letter to the editor. I won't read the article to you as you read it before I sent the letter to the paper. Now everyone will hear about the illegal land-grabbing actions of the giant cattle ranchers in the Sweetwater Valley. I'm on the side of the homesteaders who want to divide Carbon County into two smaller counties. The southern half could be for farming. And did I ever set things straight about the Town of Bothwell. The one building in the so-called town is the newspaper which he owns. That is a joke. I 'm proud that I signed James Averell, February 7, 1889

"Jim, won't you get into more trouble with the big ranchers? They're spreading rumors about us."

"Folks understand those rumors aren't true. Don't worry. The law is on our side. We're proving up our Homestead claims, and our 329 acres are top-notch land and water. You have a small herd and mine all grazing on the two homesteads. We can get a small profit if the prices for beef stay up. That winter we had killed off so many, the prices should be high for the next two or three years. We're doing everything legal. We're in the right."

"And Bothwell thinks he is in the right," said Ellen.

"Humph!"

SKULL AND CROSSBONES

CHAPTER FIFTEEN

"Boys, Jim and I appreciate it when you come to the road ranch to help when your chores are finished at home," said Ellen as she walked beside John as they sauntered home from Jim's road ranch.

A clump of dirt shot up as John kicked his foot. "There's always food to eat."

"John, you're 13, and like other boys your age, you never fill up." Ellen laughed.

A pony swished its tail as Gene walked his roan beside Ellen and John. "Yeah, John, you could eat a whole buffalo in one serving, tail and all." Gene snickered.

"You wait, Gene. You're eleven, but someday the teen appetite will hit you, too," said Ellen. "How is your leg? Does riding, instead of walking, help?"

"Ya, since my leg never healed after it broke when I was a kid. Riding takes the weight off my leg, and besides, riding is fun. I'm going to beat you back to the cabin," said Gene as he tightened his thigh muscles, and the pony sprung into a trot.

"That's not fair, Ellen," said John with a pout on his face.

"Yes, but I'm pleased to see him happy. And you, too." Ellen tousled John's hair.

Stepping to the side while laughing, John pointed. "Hey, Gene is coming back."

Waving his hat, Gene yelled, "Ellen, Ellen."

Ellen and John stopped. Gene's pony cantered up, swirling dust into the air.

"Gene, what's the matter?"

"The door of the cabin. Someone painted a skull and crossbones on it."

"Did you see anyone?"

"No."

"We're close to the house. You boys stay here while I'm going to check out the cabin." Ellen lifted her skirt higher and jogged toward the house.

The green door stood out in the setting sun's shadow. She slowed to a hesitant walk as she approached the door and touched the skull and bones in white paint. The tackiness told her the painter might be close. Opening the door, she noticed nothing was missing or disturbed. She hugged the outside wall as she slid out the door after grabbing the Winchester from the pegs. Pressing against the side of the cabin, she walked back toward the bar, and dashed across the yard, which separated the two buildings. Taking a deep breath at the barn door, she opened the single entrance next to the animal door; she peered in, and she inched her way inside. Stepping out of the light silhouetting her in the doorway and giving her eyes time to adjust to the dark interior, she stood for a moment. The rafter swallows were cooing and flapping their wings near the roof. Her heartbeat, pounding in her ears, slowed as she realized the swallows were not upset. She examined each stall as she walked cautiously down the aisle.

Leaving the barn by the back door, she scanned the pasture and corral where two horses and the milk cow grazed. In the distance, she saw the small herd of cattle that she had purchased and branded. The chickens clucked, and the geese pecked in the dirt.

Ellen examined the house door again, and the paint was dry. She walked up the road until she sighted the boys. After waving them to come, she went to the barn shed and found paintbrushes and green paint.

*　　*　　*

A week later, two cowpokes tied their broncs at the hitching posts in front of Averell's road ranch. The horses slurped at the water trough. Taking off their Stetson, they entered the wood-planked building and walked up to the bar. They heard voices in the kitchen.

"Jim, I still wish you had not mailed your letter to the editor of the Casper Weekly Mail," said Ellen. "The boys and I painted over the skull and crossbones last week, but when we got home late yesterday, there was blood smeared over the door. We scrubbed as much of it off as we could, but we likely will need to paint it again." After closing the wood stove oven door, Ellen said, "Maybe we should sell and go someplace else."

"Cowards do those sorts of things. They try to scare us. Many people become angry, but they do nothing, except maybe Bothwell. He's slicker than a rattle snake slithering on a wet hill. And he connives others to slither with him."

"That may be, but I don't enjoy seeing skulls and crossbones painted on the door of my house. It is scary, Jim, scary," said Ellen.

"Hey! Can we get a drink out here?" One of the bronc riders yelled.

Jim walked to the bar and said back over his shoulder to Ellen, "A little paint or blood doesn't hurt anyone. The cattlemen are just trying to scare us. We've worked too hard and survived through tough times to start over." Turning back to the bar area, he asked, "What would you fellas want?"

"We've been chawing rawhide for a few days. Cain't tell you when we've had real coffee."

"Sit right over there, and Ellen will serve you the best coffee and meal you've ever had." James poked his head into the backroom before saying, "Ellen, you got customers."

Ellen came out from the kitchen. Walking to the table, she said, "Howdy. I've got Pork Snow Birds for twenty-five cents; if you just want coffee, it's five cents."

The two men looked at each other. Shuffling their feet, they both glanced away. One man cleared his throat. "We ain't been paid a while. We'll take the coffee."

"Two meals and two coffees coming up. No one leaves my table hungry. I'll be back shortly."

"We can't take charity, misses. Ain't our nature."

"You've helped others out, haven't you and likely will again?"

"Yeah, but that's different."

"No, it ain't."

HARD NEWS

CHAPTER SIXTEEN

"Howdy there, Tom. Sit for a while on the porch." John Durbin turned his head and yelled, "Emma, Tom Sun came over. Bring out a jug. "Tom and me want to jaw awhile."

After Tom got off his horse, tied the reins to the hitching rail, his boots struck the board floor of the porch. "Thanks John Henry. Hoped I would find you at home. How did you fare during winter last year? It sure was an awful one."

"Yeah, I figure I lost 26,000 head of cattle. Fortunately, enough survived, so after they breed a year or two, I'll be back to where I was afore. How about you?"

"Not as well. I figure I lost near half my herd. It'll take longer to rebuild. It's a glad thing we have the Wyoming Stock Growers Association, and the law says unbranded maverick cattle are to be round up and sold to the highest bidder. The small nesters won't be able to buy many cattle. And I brought 4,000 head from Oregon. I figure with my three million acres, I'll have a decent size herd back in time."

"Yeah, I just sent some of my hands off to the Oregon Trail route. The wagon trains will travel on soon. I reckon they have left St. Louis and are getting' near Independence Rock. Their milk cows and their few herds of beef will be plum wore out. My men will offer one fat cow for two of their weak, skinny ones. After a year of grazing, they will fill my herd just fine." John Henry rocked in his chair.

Emma stepped out onto the porch and handed her husband his jug of whiskey.

Tom tipped his hat. How do, Missus?"

Emma smiled and said, "Howdy, Mr. Sun. How be Mary Agnes?"

"She is doing better now. We lost our little two-year- old. We hope to have more children someday."

"I'm so deeply sorry for the loss you have suffered. It's a heavy burden to have. I'm right, sorry. Give Mary Agnes my regards," said Emma.

"Thanks, I'll tell her. How are your two daughters and four boys doing?"

"All are doin' fine. Keeping their Ma busy, that's for sure." Emma smiled and stepped back into the house.

Taking the jug of whiskey, John Durbin continued, "With my Platte Valley Packing company up and running in Denver and my gold mine in South Dakota bringing out a fair amount of gold, soon I'll be sitting high on the hog. Have you found a new foreman to replace Tom Collins? It's a shame the Wyoming Stock Growers Association made you fire him because of his cattle rustling."

"Yeah," said Tom before he gulped a drink. "Hated to do it. He found calves that weren't branded. Don't know if the Association figured he was adding to my herd or not, but they caught him increasing his herd, so he had to go. They like getting money when they sell the unbranded calves. But we all bypass that idea by adding calves to our herds directly from the range when we can find them. My new guy is Boney Ernest. We scouted together years back. Good guy. How about your range boss, Clabe Young?"

"It's too bad he was wanted in Texas for murder and was arrested by Finkbone fella. Haven't heard how that came out, but I sure could use his talents," said John.

"I worry about the small ranchers. They are claiming and fencing off the rangeland. Averill ranch is right where he can control the tributaries of the Snake River. If we have a drought, you, me and the other ranchers will suffer. He can cut off the water we need."

"Did you read what Averill wrote in a letter to the Casper Weekly Mail?" asked John.

"No,"

"He criticized Bothwell, you know Bothwell claims the land Averill's and Watson's homesteads is his, and he says those two are stealing his cattle. He says Averill is attempting to organize the small ranchers in opposing us. Averill is getting more power. He has just been appointed the postmaster by the governor." Durbin took the jug from Tom.

"Bothwell sure won't like that. Hope he does nothing rash."

"Perhaps it's time for the big ranchers to get together and decide what we should do to protect ourselves and our property. I'll send out word to Bothwell, McLean, Galbraith, Conner, and with you and me, we'll solve the problem before the land gets carved up into small pieces," said John as he handed the jug back to Tom.

After taking a drink, Tom said," Great. Let's do it. Send me word as to when and where." Tom handed the jug to John and got on his horse and rode toward his ranch.

CHAPTER SEVENTEEN

"Okay, we're all here. Thanks for coming over to my ranch. I bought the 76 Ranch, and now I've made it into the Broken Box and the TW, which are two of the largest, so I figured we should meet here."

All eyes were on Bothwell. Tom Sun and McLean moved their eyes to the side as each thought, *He loves bragging. He wants us to know he's the biggest frog in the puddle.*

"We are the largest cattle ranchers, but it won't be for long. I fenced in a section of the open range to be the pasture for my beeves, and that Averell fella took down my fence as he said it was illegal and he homesteaded 160 acres and fenced it in. Until he came along, I controlled all the land and water for twenty miles. I made it profitable. Now, he puts a road ranch right in the middle of my land. I spent a vast amount of money putting up barbed wire fences, buying cattle and horses, and I put cowhands to work. I've been here first long before the government got interested in this land. Now, they don't care if I own the land. First come first served, right?"

"True," "That's right," "You got that right," voices of the men chimed in .

"Now Averell got that woman, Watson, to homestead on Horse Creek and get the water rights, so now she can irrigate her land and our cattle can't get to water. It's obvious the government doesn't know right from wrong. The nesters will soon put us out of business. We all know it. What are we going to do about it?" Albert waved his left arm at the men as he right held a glass of whiskey. Each of the five men had their drinks in hand.

"Tom, you own the Hub and Spoke Ranch. What do you say?"

"I thought we were buying the farmers out. Seems like we have spent a plenty of pesos to rid ourselves of the nesters," said Tom.

"Dang sure, but some won't sell. Not at any price. My cattle on the EM Bar ranch will be squeezed out by the small guys that run just a couple of heads. This Averell fella has a small ranch, but it's in a strategic spot for controlling the Sweetwater River . We need that water if there's a drought," said McLean. He took a drink of his whiskey.

"That James Averell has the ear of the small ranchers. He tells them we don't own the open range, which we all know we need. He says they can fence off their acreage for grazing and raising crops. Any fool knows the land isn't good farming. It's too dry," said Galbraith

Bob Conner spoke up. "Averell is getting support. Governor Thomas Moonlight made him a notary public in Carbon County and postmaster for the Sweetwater Post Office. On top of that, he is the justice of the peace. You're right, Galbraith, the small ranchers listen to him. Now he has that road ranch for travelers and cowmen."

"You mean rustlers, don't you? I bet if we looked at his herd, we would find our missing cattle there," said Durbin. If we look at the cattle in Averell's pasture and Watson's, I think we will find ours mixed in with theirs. My brand with the UT can be changed. A two and ½ million-acre ranch is hard to patrol."

"Do you really think they're rustling?" asked Galbraith.

"Absolutely," said two ranchers together.

"My foreman was a stock detective, so he could go to the two ranches and report his findings to us. If he finds they are rustlers hiding behind legal businesses, we will have a reason to act." Durbin put his empty glass on the table.

Bothwell filled it up.

All the men talked at once and agreed Durbin had a great idea.

"It's unanimous that your foreman, ah, what's his name?" said Bothwell.

"George Henderson."

"It's unanimous that George Henderson a stock detective and boss man of the Quarter Circle 71, will scout out the Averell and Watson ranches and report back to us about these two rustlers. If it's okay with you, Durbin, your man can report directly to me, as my ranch is closest to the nesters' ranches instead of going back to your ranch, as your place is so far from the rest of us," said Albert Bothwell.

"That's fine with me," said John Durbin.

"Once I hear from Henderson, we can meet again and decide from there," said Bothwell.

"If everything is settled, I'm headed home because, as you said, I have a fair piece to go." Durbin downed his drink and stood.

The other men grabbed their hats and followed him out the door.

*　　*　　*

A chestnut gelding halted at the hitching rail and water trough. The rider dismounted. His boots pounded on the board porch, then on the floor of the roadhouse. The door was open, letting in customers with the dust and flies. Walking over to the bar, made of two rough planks of wood laid from end to end on upright barrels, he said, "Whiskey." He put down two-bits on the bar. "Can a cowpoke get grub here? No pork and beans. No trail food."

"Sure thing. Ellen is a wonderful cook. Today, she made salt pork in milk gravy with cooked onions served with cornbread, and topped off with coffee, all for twenty-five cents. I serve only beer. Good nuff?" Jim walked back to the kitchen area and called Ellen.

"Yeah. This place being a road ranch you have stock. How many head do you run?"

"I got about 400 and Ellen bought 250."

"Can folks spend the night?"

"Sure can. Ten cents."

"If, say, a fella wants a little companionship, do you provide that as well?"

"No, sir, you got to bring the hussy yourself."

"Okay, I'll take a meal. My bronc needs shade while I eat."

"Yep. Over by the barn in the back. A stand of trees, water, and tall grass. You can take the saddle off. No one will steal it."

"Thanks." George took a drink of beer.

"Say, what's your name? I haven't seen you around here before," said Jim.

"Henderson, George Henderson."

"Welcome, George. Hope you like it in these parts."

"I reckon I will." After leaving the bar, Henderson untied his cayuse and walked around to the corral. Removing the saddle, he hobbled the bay's front legs and poked his head into the barn. Noticing four horses in a corral out the open back door, he stepped inside.

A boy bent lower than the wall of the stall was laying fresh hay down. He stood and spotted George. "Can I help you, mister?" Henderson's head jerked back as the boy surprised him. "Ah... Ah...I was looking for something to wipe the sweat from my mare."

"The box on the left side of the door holds brushes, combs, hoof picks, and anything else you might need." The boy pointed in the box's direction. "My name is Gene Crowder. What's yours?"
"Henderson."

"Glad to meet you. I hope you eat Ellen's victuals. She cooks real fine."

"Yeah, I'm fixing to chow down after I wipe down my horse." George turned and walked over to his chestnut. Keeping one eye on the boy and the stalls, he scanned the horizon. *No one else appears to be around. Don't see any cattle or hands.*

*   *   *

After eating, George saddled his mare and trotted to Ellen's place. The barn was empty. Seeing no one around the corral, he headed to the back. Later, he rode to the top of a grassy hill. Wheeling his mount, we went below the rim. Dismounting, he took binoculars from his saddlebags and walked to the crest. He lay on his stomach and peered over the edge.

The area below had four cowpunchers and a small herd of cattle. He estimated about 600. Scanning through his binoculars at the animals' flanks as they grazed, he laid for hours, staring at the brands. By night fall, he had counted only two. Didn't see any brands from the six ranchers. *But that ain't what Bothwell wants to hear. I'll tell him there were two brands. He can decide if they're rustling cattle.* He slid off the hill's rim, mounted his chestnut, and rode toward the Bothwell TW Ranch.

*   *   *

"You be Mr. Bothwell?" A mustached man in a worn slouch hat rode up to a man walking near the house on the TW Ranch.

"Yes, Who are you?"

"George Henderson, Mr. Durbin sent me to inspect the Watson and Averell ranches for stolen cattle."

"And what did you find?"

"I found two different brands on the beefs. Might be theirs."

"I'll tell the others that different brands were found on Ellen Watson's property, and Jim Averell's I won't say how many brands or whose they might belong to. Those two people are holding us up with plans to expand. They won't sell, so need to run them off. Come in, and I'll give you some traveling money. It would be a good idea if you left these parts. Say, go to Cheyenne, which is 150 miles."

"Cheyenne suits me fine."

"Inform me where you will be staying. When I send you a telegram, open this envelope containing instructions. I wrote everything out. Once you receive the telegram from me, burn the instructions. A bag of hefty dinero for you if you do things right. Get my drift?"

"Sure do, Mr. Bothwell. I'll be glad to help you out."

"Here is traveling money and expenses." Albert Bothwell handed George two hundred dollars.

* * *

At the Sweetwater Chief Paper, the only building in the town of Bothwell. Mr. Fetz was stacking the paper for the printing press when Mr. Speer, his partner, walked in.

"Hey Speer, I heard we can see something spectacular tomorrow. We need to be up on the roof with binoculars and scan Bothwell's. Something newsworthy may happen.

"Who said that?"

"Well, this is the place Bothwell calls a town he has named for himself, and he hired us to come and start the paper. So, you can guess who the informant is."

"Okay, sounds top-notch. Let's watch."

CHAPTER EIGHTEEN

"Okay, Bothwell, we are all here." In the distance, they heard a horse, so they turned in their saddles. "Oh, sorry, Tom Sun is coming across the hayfield. I heard he got a new buggy with front and back seats. Sure looks spiffy." The men waited as Tom drove his carriage up to the group. "Hi Tom."

Reining in the horse, Tom said, "Hi everyone. Got the message. Why are we meeting? And why here in your meadow, Bothwell?"

Bothwell took out two whiskey bottles and passed them around. "Ellen Watson and Jim Averell filed their last claim on my land. It's my land by rights. I've been using this section for years." Bothwell gulped whiskey before giving it to Tom. "Henderson reported to me he found cattle with more than one brand in their pastures. One brand is registered to Averell, but the other isn't. The two are in it together. Are you men standing with me in driving these two rustlers out? I've tried to buy them out at a huge profit, but neither will sell."

The two bottles go from man to man. The ranchers tossed the drained bottles on the prairie grass. Bothwell took out another bottle. "Averell writes a scathing article in the Casper Weekly Mail and riles up the homesteaders. He calls me a cheat. Come with me to Watson's place and observe for yourself. They have been rustling and branding cattle. McLean, Galbraith, Durbin, Conner, and Sun, I know you will join me in getting rid of them once and for all?"

"I don't like the nesters, same as you, Bothwell, but I don't want any rough stuff. No killing. But I'm with you on driving them out," said Tom.

"Well, let's see for ourselves. If we don't notice any cattle with the wrong brands on them, all is well. But if we do, we need to act." Bothwell moved his horse forward, and the others followed behind his lead.

* * *

Mr. Speer and Mr. Fetz climbed onto the newspaper's building roof. They scanned the hay meadow with binoculars. They could see Ellen's and Jim's ranches.

"Hey, wondering what the cattlemen are doing in Bothwell's hay field?"

"Yeah, and now they're riding off toward Watson's place "

"This looks really interesting."

* * *

Meadow Larks twittered in the tall prairie grass. The sun passed the midday point.

"John, did you have fun playing with the Shoshonean boys?" Ellen glanced down at her beaded moccasin feet.

"Sure did. Glad you took me with you to the village. I wish Gene had felt like coming."

"Perhaps another time. These moccasins are so beautiful I couldn't resist buying them."

The hay swished in the light breeze as the two traipsed from the Shoshone village through Bothwell's hayfield to Ellen's ranch.

John stopped when Ellen stopped without warning. She was staring at the cabin. A strained look replaced her smile.

"What's going on at the ranch? Two of our horses are tied to the back of that buggy. Hey, men are tearing down my fence and running the cattle out," said Ellen. The two broke into a run.

Before Ellen arrived at her ranch, Durbin began yanking out the nails from the fence posts and pulled the barbed wire down. The cabin door burst open, and Gene ran out. "Hey, stop that. You're wrecking everything. Stop!"

"Kid, go back into the house, or we'll take care of you, too," Bothwell growled.

After fleeing into the house, Gene slid the bolt on the door and barricaded it. Going to a window, he peered out.

Ellen and John reached the cabin, and the men surrounded Ellen. They all talked at the same time, accusing her of stealing cattle and rebranding them. She screamed above their voices. "I have a bill of sale. The cattle are mine. They have my brand on them."

"Show us the bill of sale. Show us."

"It's in the Rawlins Bank. I can show it to you tomorrow. They are my cattle, paid for."

"We don't believe you. You're a nester, a liar, a rustler and a harlot at that so-called road ranch."

"I'm not. I cook. That's all. The cattle are mine. Bothwell, you've seen the cattle on my ranch for a year now. Tell them."

I haven't seen any such thing. You stole them. You can't afford to buy so many. Not over forty head."

"I bought twenty-eight from an immigrant named Engerman. They were footsore, and he sold them at a dollar a head. The pregnant ones gave birth in the spring."

John pulled and punched with his calloused hands at Bothwell. Bothwell pushed him to the ground.

Gene came out and bolted over to his pony, jumped on its bareback, and tried to run over the cattlemen at the gate.

Bothwell jumped in front of the running pony, grabbed its halter, and spun it around. Then he pulled Gene down. "Kid, stand by Durbin and help him run the calves out of the corral."

His legs trembled as he followed orders.

"Watson, you climb into the back of Tom's buggy and don't move."

"Why? Where are we going?"

"To Rawlins, to put you on the train," said Tom Sun.

"Let me go in and change clothes. These aren't proper clothes to wear in town or on a train."

"Where you're going, you won't need any fancy clothes. Now get in, or I'll tie you behind and drag you." Bothwell grabbed Ellen's arm and shoved her into the back seat as the men mounted their horses. They headed for Jim's ranch.

The horse galloped forward with the buggy and its occupants bouncing. Within minutes, they arrived at Averell's place.

Jim, carrying buckets headed to the barn, stopped. The commotion of the riders caused him to turn and glare at the mob. He flinched when he sighted tears streaming down Ellen's face. Without his gun or rifle, he knew he had to stay calm and not provoke the men. "What do you want?" "We have a warrant for your arrest," said Bothwell with authority.

"Let me see it."

"Rifles are warrant enough," said Bothwell as he and Conner pulled their Winchesters from their sheaths. "Climb in the buggy."

With steady steps, Jim walked to the wagon and got in.

"Tom, drive around the cabin and away from the road ranch so no one will see us," said Conner.

The wagon bounced off at top speed, and the riders cantered behind. As soon as they left, Gene Crowder and John DeCorey got some cattle back into the pasture and set up the fence as best as they could. Gene's horse had run off, so running for a mile, they raced to Jim's road ranch.

Bursting through the door, they gasped out to Ralph Cole and Frank Buchanan what happened. Frank grabbed his gun, holster, cartridge belt and charged out the door. He put the bit in his horse's mouth, saddled, tightened the cinch and galloped across the sagebrush for a mile before he spotted the carriage. He followed, staying out of sight. Bothwell's words drifted up to his ears, "Let's drown the two if they don't promise to leave the country today."

He heard Ellen laugh. "There ain't enough water in the whole Sweetwater to give even a dirty land hog a bath."

"Okay then, let's go to where this shallow river veers into the Spring Creek Culch. We'll see what you say then missy," said John Durbin.

Off the carriage careened as before. Tom followed Bothwell and the others as they rode their mounts at a gallop. Ellen and Jim held tight to the buggy until their knuckles were white, as it bounced and flew over the rocky terrain.

Frank Buchanan followed and when men stopped by boulders at Spring Creek Gulch, he dismounted on the other side of a ridge. He let the reins dangle as his boots scraped on the steep and rocky climb. Near the top of the ridge, he lay on his belly and peered over the edge.

At the gulch, the men tied their horses to green junipers. Bothwell pulled out and passed around another whiskey bottle. Feeling the whiskey effects, the men forced Ellen and Jim out of the buggy and onto a boulder under a pine tree branch. They threw two ropes over the limb.

Forced onto the top of the rock, the two captives struggled and fought. Even though Jim's hands were not tied, the men put a noose around his neck as he fought.

"Let's see if they are willing to sell now," said Tom.

Ellen squirmed and twisted around, hit and scratched, but finally, they got the noose around her neck.

They really are going to do it. Maybe this will scare them off. Frank took aim with his revolver and fired. Durbin, at that moment, moved into where Frank aimed.

Hit in the hip, Durbin fell as he screamed. He writhed on the ground.

The ranchers grabbed their rifles and fired toward the rocks. Dust and rock chips flew as the bullets hit the boulders. Frank ducked below eyesight. In the turmoil, Ellen screamed as Jim slipped off the boulder, twisted and turned, trying desperately to make his feet touch something. Anything! But nothing.

Ellen's screams echoed through the gulch. The men, half dazed with whisky, watched Jim struggle. He reached out to Ellen, grabbed onto her and she was pulled off the boulder.

The tree shivered, and the branch shook and bent but did not break.

Ellen twisted and kicked her legs in a desperate attempt to find a ledge or rock to stand on. Her toes could almost touch the boulder. She flung out her feet and strained to force them on something solid. Her moccasins flew off and landed on the ground.

The victims twisted and turned, bumping into each other, grabbing at each other, gouging at each other, trying to relieve the pressure around their necks and throats. The thin hemp of the rope cut into their skin. They could not reach behind them to pull themselves up.

Their tongues swelled; their eyes bulged. Blood came from their noses and mouths as they made gurgling sounds. They kept twisting and kicking for an unmerciful time. Then, nothing. The breeze blew dust around on the ground and in the air. Wind ruffled Ellen's hair and skirt and Jim's shirt.

Six men stared with gaping mouths at the silent pair. A slight smile showed on Bothwell's face.

Durbin bit his lower lip as the pain engulfed him. He. thought, *Now I'm shot because of those two. They shouldn't have gotten my*

Irish temper up. They had a simple time to get land while I had to struggle. They should have sold.

His chest heaved up and down as if he had been running. He pulled off a neckerchief as he stuffed it against his bleeding hip. *The pain is killing me. I need to get to a doctor, all because of them.* "Fellas, I'm leaving. I need a doctor." The men helped Durbin up from the ground. He slowly mounted and rode toward the distant train tracks.

Conner gawked at the two. *If they had been reasonable and sold their property, this wouldn't have happened. They asked for it. There is no going back for them, but they don't matter anyway.* He made a wide stance and crossed his arms.

I just wanted to belong to the power group The big guys. That's all. The thoughts flooded McLean's brain. He looked away from the ghastly sight. He swallowed hard several times to keep the bile down.

Tom Sun turned away and walked to his buggy. He got on the seat and took up the reins as he said, "They should have sold out to us. It's survival out here. Nothing is easy. We need their land. We can't expand our holdings with sodbusters in the way. They should have known better. We gave them plenty of warning." He clucked to his horse and slapped the reins, and the horse pulled the carriage forward. His voice sounded like he was trying to convince himself. Tom turned his back to the swinging couple.

Without a word, the other men mounted their horses and rode off in their separate ways, except Conner and Bothwell.

"Hey, Conner, let's go back to the Watson's ranch and take their cattle for ourselves," said Bothwell.

"Sounds good."

The two men rode to Ellen's ranch while her body swayed on the tree. At the ranch, they finished tearing down the fence and chased out the cattle. After dividing them, they headed to their ranches.

*   *   *

Mr. Fetz and Mr. Speer climbed off the roof. In the office, they eyed each other silently. They closed up the newspaper office.

SORRY OR NOT

CHAPTER NINETEEN

Frank left his stakeout position and gallop to Jim's ranch. Halting at the hitching rail, he called out to John, Gene and Ralph. They rushed out. Each gasped with lips stretched and drawn back. They had raised eyebrows with an intense stare.

Without dismounting, Frank yelled, "They were hung. Both of them. They're dead. I'm going to get the sheriff in Casper." He galloped off without a look back.

Three faces stared after Frank for a moment before erupting into sobs.

Frank rode most of the night to Tex Healy's shack. His horse covered in a sweaty foam, its rider heaved, and its legs trembled in exhaustion, stopped at the hitching rail. Frank blurted out to Tex what had happened.

"Your horse won't make it all the way to Casper. Its tuckered out. You stay here while I saddle and ride to get the sheriff." Tex talked as he ran to the barn to saddle his horse.

*   *   *

The screen door screeched as it opened. Charlie Countryman stepped out on to his porch and lit his pipe. He took a breath of the hot, humid air. He scanned the sky, hoping to see rain clouds. Hearing sobbing, he gazed at the side of the porch. Seated on the step was a man convulsed in sobs.

"Hey, what do you want? Who are you?" asked Charlie.

The man stood and turned around. He leaned against a post for support. Staring straight into Charlie's eyes with his red, swollen ones, he said, "I'm Ernie McLean."

Charlie's wife and children came to the door.

"I've got to tell someone. I've got to tell. I can't keep it locked up in me," said Ernie.

"Man, you look awful. What happened?" asked Charlie.

"I need to tell what the other men and I did. I didn't think it would happen. I didn't think it would be like this."

"What happened? What did you do?"

"We just wanted them to sell their land to us. But they wouldn't do it. We asked them over and over. We warned them. They had to sell."

"Who?"

"Watson and Averell. We went to Watson's place first, grabbed her, forced her into the buggy, and next went to Averell's and got him into the carriage. With Albert Bothwell in the lead, Tom Sun drove the team wild across the rough land with the two in the back, hanging on, in fear of bouncing out. The rest of us followed on horses. We drove one way and changed to another. We tried scaring them. We said we would drown them if they didn't sell."

Mrs. Countryman scowled before she said, "You didn't drown them, did you?"

"No worse. Much worse. We stopped at Spring Creek Gulch. We forced them up onto boulders and threw ropes over a pine tree limb and got a noose around their necks. Ellen Watson fought every second. Jim pleaded we should not hang Ellen, but we didn't listen. They both slid off the boulder and strangled to death. I'll never forget. The grotesque sight is burned into my head. I had to tell somebody who wasn't there." Sobbing and gasping, his eyes pleaded for understanding, for compassion, for forgiveness.

"Get off my porch. Off my land, Now. I never want to see you again. Get off!"

Ernie's body trembled as he sobbed. He stumbled to the hitching rail, mounted his horse. He slumped in the saddle and put the horse into a walk.

*　　*　　*

Ranch hands from several ranches gathered in Bothwell's hay meadow the next morning to receive their orders for the roundup. Gene Crowder rode up to the group yelling, "I expected you all would gather here for the roundup. Do you know what happened yesterday? Ellen Watson and Jim Averell got lynched. They're dead. Why? Because they wouldn't sell their land to you, Bothwell. I saw the lynchers. You were the leader of Tom Sun, Ernie McLean, John Durbin, Cap'n Galbraith, and Bob Conner.

You murdered them."

"Bothwell, you didn't hang them, did you?" asked the cowhand, Joe Sharp.

Bothwell didn't answer. He wouldn't look anyone in the face. A moment later, without taking his eyes from looking at the ground, he wheeled his mount as he said, "Let's go. We've a roundup to do."

The cowboys mumbled under their breath as they urged their horses to follow Bothwell.

Gene sobbed. He watched the men ride off. "No one cares. No one." He turned, slumped in the saddle and rode to Ellen's place.

*　　*　　*

Tex rode up to the sheriff's house and pounded on the door. He paced back and forth. A light snapped on in the window. The door opened, and Sheriff Watson, holding a kerosene lamp said, "What do you want this time of night?"

"Sheriff Watson, are you related to Ellen Watson?" asked Tex.

"No, Why do you ask that?"

"Sheriff, Jim Averell and Ellen Watson did the Texas Cakewalk."

"What? They hung a woman! Who did it? Where?" The sheriff stared at Tex.

"Don't know all the particulars. Frank Buchanan near rode his horse to death to get to my place. We can meet up with him and he can take us the rest of the way. He seen it happen."

"I'm goin' round up some men for a posse and grab Dr. Benson to act as coroner. It's best to do it before the bodies are too old or get buried. I need to find Justice of Peace Emery, too. He can conduct the inquest right on the spot." The sheriff put down the lamp and rushed out the door without his shirt.

*   *   *

A posse formed at the sheriff's office. The doctor had his buggy in which Justice of the Peace, Mr. Emery, rode as well.

Soon Casper's few lights disappeared behind the posse as they rode into the sweltering ebony night. Clouds lazily drifted across the moon, but it shed enough light to guide the riders.

After reaching Tex's ranch, Frank Buchanan saddle his cooled-down horse. In the humid, dark and sultry night, the posse continued on to Jim's ranch. They met the two boys and Ralph, who were working on crude pine coffins. The posse lit a couple pine knot torches, and Frank led them to the boulders at Spring Creek Gulch.

The sun was peeking over the horizon when the posse reined in and looked up.

Two bodies had been hanging in the summer heat for one- and- a- half days by the time the posse arrived. Their tongues black and hard, their eyes bulging, and their faces covered with flies where blood had seeped out of noses, ears and mouth, made the two unrecognizable.

Men in the posse said, "Tarnation," "Watch out! Russ is upchucking.", "Sakes alive."

"Men, climb up and cut them down. We'll take them to Averell's ranch," said Sheriff Watson.

With caution the men climbed up on the rocks. One man crept part way up the pine tree to reach the ropes. He cut through the ropes on the top of the branch. He had the best job. The other men held on to the bodies to catch them as the ropes released them. They made sure they touched only the clothing and not the skin.

"Men, put the bodies in the back of my carriage," said the doctor.

When the grizzly work was finished and the two bodies loaded in the back of the buggy, a member of the posse used his bedroll blanket to cover them. They headed back to Averell's ranch.

Jim's nephew, Robert Cole, and Ellen's two boys, Gene and John had been up all night making two coffins. They gawk at the bloated bodies, then sobbed openly. The stench of the rotting flesh filled the room. They placed each body in a separate coffin. A posse member nailed the lids down.

"Come on, men Let's dig a grave. Make it deep enough for the two of them.

The posse went out and, with shovels they found in the barn, they dug about five feet down where they hit water flowing in from Horse Creek. They lowered the coffins and Frank said words over the grave. Each person put a shovel of dirt on the boxes. The thud of the wet soil hitting the wood made a sickening sound that matched the horrid smell. They stood two oak wagon wheels upright as markers.

"Frank, who did this?" Sheriff Watson led the posse out to the stabled horses.

"Albert Bothwell, Tom Sun, Bob Conner, John Henry Durbin, Robert Galbraith and Ernest McLean. They were all in on it."

"We'll get them. No worries about that." Sheriff Phil Watson rode with the posse across the dry land to Tom Sun's ranch.

The sheriff dismounted and walked up to the door. He pounded on it until Tom came out. "Tom Sun, I'm here to arrest you for the murders of Jim Averell and Ellen Watson."

"Yes, I did it and so did others. It needed to be done, as they were cattle rustlers. I'm glad to go with you." Tom went to the barn, saddled his horse, and rode with the posse to Albert Bothwell's ranch. The dust from the horse's hooves became thick and covered the animals' legs.

At Al Bothwell's ranch, Al came out on his porch. "What do you all want here?"

"Mr. Bothwell, we're here to arrest you for the hanging of Watson and Averell."

"Yeah, I and some others did it. It had to be done. They were cattle thieves. I'll go with you after I write out a message I want to send by telegraph. I'll send it with a cowhand into Rawlins telegraph office. It's about business in Cheyenne."

"Okay, but hurry it up," said the sheriff.

After Bothwell handed the stable hand an envelope, and mounted his horse, the posse continued to all the ranches and picked up the men, except for John Durbin, who was not at home.

The sun licked the sky as the tired men and horses proceeded back to Averell's ranch. A sultry breeze plagued the posse.

"Judge Emery, good thing you are part of the posse. We can hold a coroner's inquest right now."

"You're right. Let's hold it in the barn." Justice of the Peace, Judge Emery from Casper, led the way to the barn. It had shelter from the solar blaze, yet it was stifling and breathless.

Men set up a table for the judge. He sat on a bale of hay. The other men stood around the table or leaned on the walls of the stalls. The air bristled with excitement. Everyone knew the names of the defendants.

"Doctor, will you write the proceedings?" asked Judge Emery.

"Certainly." The doctor scrounged up paper and a pencil from the house. When he returned, the judge banged a gun butt on the table.

"This is an inquest in James Averell and Ellen Watson's deaths on July 20, 1889. The jury will be the posse and is assembled. The charged men are present. Any witnesses to the crime?"

"Yes, Judge. My name is Frank Buchanan."

"Do you take the oath to tell the truth?"

"Yes, I do."

"Go ahead."

"I seen Albert Bothwell, Tom Sun, Ernest McLean, Bob Conner, John Durbin and Robert Galbraith put ropes around the necks of James Averell and Ellen Watson. I shot Durbin in the hip. They returned fire, so I took off and rode to Tex Healy's place and he rode to Casper for help."

Several men removed their Stetsons and wiped the sweatbands with bandanas. Some fanned themselves with their hats.

"Are there other witnesses?"

"Yes, John DeCory, and Gene Crowder, Ella Watson's two children."

"Boys, do you swear to Almighty God to tell the truth?" Gene and John looked at each other and said in unison, "I do."

"What do you boys say?"

"We saw those men sitting over there, force Ellen into the buggy and took off with her. She didn't want to go, but they made her. They headed for Jim's ranch. Later, we seen the bodies of Jim and Ella when we buried them." John spoke, and Gene nodded Ralph stepped forward. "Judge, my name is Ralph Cole. I'm the nephew of Jim Averell."

"Are you a witness, and if so, do you swear to tell the truth?" "I do. I was at the ranch when Gene and John came and told me about Ella being taken. I went to find my uncle. He was missing. Tracks showed a wagon stopped, and boot prints told the story of Jim being forced into the buggy."

"Gene, John, and Ralph did any of you see the actual hanging?" asked the Judge.

"No, but we know it was those men," said Ralph as Gene and John echoed his words.

"What do the six men say?" asked Judge Emery.

"Judge, you know me. I'm Albert Bothwell. I swear to tell the truth. Speaking for the other men, I can tell you those two nesters were rustlers. Averell was a murderer; he killed a man named Charlie Johnson by shooting him in the back and Watson ran a bawdy house as well. We had to protect our property. We had the right."

The other cattle men said, "That's right.", "Dang right.", That's the truth."

"If that is all the witnesses, I set bail for the six defendants at five thousand greenbacks each and after they meet bail, they may return to their ranches or homes in Cheyenne until the trial."

"Judge, can we pay for each other's bail?" asked Al Bothwell. "Yes," said the Judge. "This inquest is closed."

GUILTY OR NOT

CHAPTER TWENTY

After opening the telegram sent by Bothwell, George Henderson read he was to open the letter of instruction Bothwell had given him before he took the train to Cheyenne.

The instructions were, 'Head to the newspaper's offices and inform them that Cattle Kate, also known as Ellen Watson, and the cattle thief and murderer James Averell were hanged. Their reign of terror is over.' After reading the letter burn it and the telegram.' Once he read the instructions, he burned the two pieces of paper and brushed the ashes out of his hotel window. Then he rushed over to the Cheyenne Daily Leader. He entered the office smiling. "I have a story for the reporter and editor, Edward Towse. "The Wyoming Stock Growers Association owned the paper, so George knew he would have no problem convincing Towse to print what he was told. A few minutes later, he left the offices, chuckling to himself.

* * *

Edward Towse printed the story in the Cheyenne Daily Leader making Ellen Watson a prostitute, and cattle thief, and James Averell a drunken pimp, murderer, and cattle thief. The cattle men who hung the two acted in self-protection for their lives and property.

The other newspapers followed the lead of the Cheyenne Daily Leader and even embellished the stories. Soon Ellen was known as the infamous Cattle Kate.

* * *

A servant in a white vest, black cut-away coat, wearing white gloves, held a silver tray with newspapers. Shiny black shoes completed his attire as he delivered the papers to Samuel Finch at the Cheyenne Cattlemen's Club in Cheyenne.

Mr. and Mrs. Finch were having coffee on the verandah. They had been talking about the upcoming dress ball. Mr. Finch began reading the newspaper.

"Hey, see this in 'The Cheyenne Sun Newspaper.' You've heard about Jim Averell and Ellen Watson."

"Sure. All the ladies have. They are the worse of the nesters, and all our husbands, including you, want them out. They are a bad influence on the other small ranchers. What does the paper say?"

"Edward Slack writes for the Cheyenne Sun and he wrote that Averell and Watson were ruthless criminals who have been a threat to the folks in Sweetwater Valley for years. 'It reads the honest people have been in constant fear for their lives.'" Mr. Finch continued, "My, gosh the paper says Albert Bothwell, John Durbin and Tom Sun are examples of shining citizenry in ridding us of these two murders. It says Averell was the ringleader of the cattle-rustling, and he murdered a man named Charlie Johnson in 1880." Samuel read to his wife between sips of coffee.

He continued reading and then told his wife what he read. "The sun goes on about Ellen Watson, a daredevil in the saddle, handy with a six-shooter, and handy with a branding iron. She also rode straddle like a man, always had a vicious horse for a mount, and dashed across the range. Slack reports Watson was a prostitute and running a bawdy house and gambling den. She and Averell were a cause of life and death between honest men and cutthroat thieves."

"I'm glad the paper put the story in for the law-abiding citizens to read. I don't think most folks around here know what a threat those two were living so close to the up-standing cattle ranches. They should know the small ranchers would have to be rustlers. Of course, they were outlaws. They couldn't possibly make enough money to survive on the small acres they had if they didn't do rustling." Mrs. Finch poured cream into her coffee.

Sam Finch picked up another paper. "'The Cheyenne Daily Leader' says about the same thing. The reporter, Edward Towse, wrote the article he called 'A double Lynching'. He describes the crimes the two committed. He also says Ellen Watson was Cattle Kate."

Mrs. Finch stopped sipping, swallowed, and said, "I've been hearing about her for years. So she was that notorious outlaw.

Imagine that. Living right here in the Sweetwater area. Well, good riddance is all I've got to say. The men who hung that pair of no-goods saved us all. They are heroes. Cattle raisers can't sit idly by while their property is being stolen. They have to act, of course." She put down her coffee cup. "Oh, some ladies are coming in who I want to talk with about the formal ball later this week. Talk to you later, dear." Standing, she put her linen napkin on the table and sashayed to the four women who had just entered the club.

"I'm glad you're all here. Let's discuss the ball." Mrs. Finch said as she laid her hand on the first woman's arm. "Let's go into the Ladies Salon and visit."

"We were discussing the ball as we came in the door. We're sure the Durbins won't be able to come."

"Why can't they come?" Mrs. Finch followed the ladies into the parlor.

"Didn't you hear? A rustler shot John in the hip. He had to ride his horse all the way to Rawlins and then take a train to his home here in Cheyenne. He must have been in terrible pain."

The ladies all agreed and nodded their sympathies.

"We were also wondering who Albert Bothwell will escort to the dance, "said one of the ladies as she sat on an embroidered cushioned straight-back chair.

"Why, Mrs. Bothwell, of course," said Mrs. Finch.

"My dear, haven't you heard?" A second woman opened her fan and held it close to her mouth. "Margaretta packed up her two children by her first marriage and went to California to get a divorce."

"No."

"Yes. She had no choice if you ask me. Not with Albert flashing that photograph around to the men here at the Club of his twin baby girls he had with his ranch housekeeper, Miss Wadsworth. Of course Margaretta found out and I understand she saw the photograph."

"No." Mrs. Finch's eyes widened as she exhaled her no.

"Yes, indeed."

A third lady spoke. "She is partly to blame, in my opinion."

"How can you say that?" asked Mrs. Finch with a disapproving frown.

"She went out to the ranch one time. Afterward, she refused to go. She said it was too dirty, no conveniences, and the cowhands were coarse. Men have needs, you know. Albert went alone, stayed for weeks at a time, as all our husbands do at their ranches, and with a lovely house keeper, things were bound to happen."

"That's still no excuse, whatsoever. With his high-and-mighty ways and spouting of his education from Eastern schools, does not mean he can disregard society's morals. I'm going to tell my husband to have as little to do with Albert Bothwell as possible." Mrs. Finch flounced off to find Mr. Finch.

CHAPTER TWENTY-ONE

The horse trotted up to the small house owned by Mr. Speer and Mr. Fetz, editors of the Casper Weekly Mail in the Town of Bothwell. Ralph Cole dismounted and knocked on the door. Mr. Speer opened it.

"Speer, can I stay with you and Fetz for a few days? The doctor at the military post told me I have the beginnings of Mountain Fever. He gave me medicine to take and said I should stay with someone until I'm well.

"Sure, come on in. Mountain Fever isn't too bad. I'll put up your horse. Make yourself ta home."

Fetz moved his things into Speer's bedroom so Ralph could have his room.

The next morning, Speer asked, "How did you sleep, Ralph?"

"Okay. There is pain in my lower back. I think I'll be fine in a few days."

In the evening, Ralph went into convulsions, which lasted about three minutes and ended up returning later. Between spasms, he said he had severe pain in his lower back.

"Speer, I'm going to ride into Casper and get Dr. Haynes. I'll be back tomorrow. Ralph is looking worse, and I don't like those convulsions he is having," said Fetz

*   *   *

Fetz found Doctor Hayes in the saloon having a drink with Bob Conner. "Doc, Ralph Cole is at my place, in a bad way. The doctor at the fort said he has Mountain Fever and gave him medicine, but he's out of the tonic now. Can you come?"

"Sure, Mountain Fever is rarely deadly for adults, but makes people mighty sick. Let's leave early in the morning. I'll stay at your place overnight. I'll bring medicine. I can leave it with you when I return to town."

"Yeah, and tell Ralph, I'll pay the doctor's fees and send along a bottle of whiskey. Often helps with the miseries." Bob Conner flipped a coin on the bar. "Here, have a drink on me."

"It's right decent of you, Conner, to help Ralph like this, seeing as he named you as one of the cattlemen who hung his Uncle Averell." Fetz lifted the glass of beer the bartender set before him.

"I don't carry grudges. Ain't in my nature. Don't want the young man sick."

*   *   *

Dr. Hayes spent the day with Ralph Cole, giving him medicine and putting hot towels on his back. Before he left the next day, he said, "Ralph is getting better. Keep giving him the medicine. I'll come back in a couple of days to see how he's feeling." The doctor packed up his medical bag, and after hitching up his buggy, he headed for town.

Fetz and Speer gave Ralph sips of the whiskey sent by Bob Conner along with the medicine. Ralph said he had less pain, but his stomach swelled.

(Note: On August 24, 1889, Ralph Cole, nephew of James Averell, died. His death was about a month after his uncle's).

ANOTHER OPINION

CHAPTER TWENTY-TWO

Mr. Countryman drove his wagon to the back door of his ranch house. His wife and children jumped down and helped him unload the groceries and supplies they had bought in Rawlins. Afterward, he drove the wagon to the barn, unhitched and pastured the horse. He walked through the back door and saw the newspapers on the table.

His wife said, "I'm glad we bought all these papers. It's been a few days since the hangings, and the *Laramie Boomerang* heard a different side to the stories which were published in *the Cheyenne Daily Leader* and *the Cheyenne Sun*."

"The Casper Mail reports that wealthy cattlemen control the Cheyenne Daily Leader, and the Cheyenne Sun. Casper Mail says the strangling of the couple was cold-blooded murder."

Charlie, using a boot jack, yanked his boots off and stretched his toes. He picked up a paper. "And the *Laramie Boomerang* wrote, 'If disputes over land matters had anything to do with the double lynchings, the paper stands by the *Casper Mail* in referring to the strangling of the couple as murder.'" The rancher took off his hat and laid it next to the newspapers on the table.

Opening the Bill Barlow's Budget, he scanned the news and stopped at the editorial. "Listen to this, ' Tex Healy, the cowboy Buchanan, and the boy, Gene Crowder, have fled to Casper for protection'. It says that 'John DeCorey went to Steamboat Springs to hide out.' And the paper flat out says, 'Ralph Cole is dead. And there is no evidence against the accused men except Buchanan's and he seems to have skipped the country. The accused parties deny having confessed to the hanging or any complicity with the matter. That settles it, Probably! Averell and Watson committed suicide, probably! Buchanan will disappear, probably, and that will end the matter- probably!' That's a direct quote from the paper. Finally, an editor is willing to show what happened. Someone is now getting people to think."

Mrs. Countryman rustled through pages of the Carbon County Journal. "This is what the paper writes, 'it is reported Averell lived with this woman Watson at one time while not married to her, but if this is sufficient cause for mob law, what a glorious field Wyoming presents for hanging parties.'"

"Here it says, 'People are raising money for another inquest with news articles coming out refuting the claims of the cattle barons.'" The rancher tipped back in his chair and smiled. "Maybe the truth will come out. But remember, we won't tell anyone what Ernie McLean said that day on the porch."

"Right, we don't want to become involved."

The two faced each other. Relief shone in their eyes. Mrs. Countryman said, "Justice. This will be over. We can sleep."

*   *   *

George Henderson strode onto Al Bothwell's porch as the sun painted a pink sky with a trace of purple. Bothwell came out to stand next to George.

"George, it looks like there will be a trial. If witnesses don't show up, no one can be found guilty. Ralph Cole conveniently died of Mountain Fever."

"With a little help from Bob Conner and strychnine in whiskey, I heard. George smiled and twisted a hay strand in his mouth.

"That's just a rumor. There is no proof." Bothwell's voice carried a strong edge, which told George to drop the idea. "Now, Frank Buchanan has posted a five-hundred-dollar bond to appear and testify. He claims he took a shot at the lynchers during the hanging and can identify them. He, of course, is making false claims about me. If Frank Buchanan turned up and convinced the jury of his lie, that wouldn't be good for several of us cattlemen. He should not implicate the wrong people. If you could arrange that he did not testify, it would be money in your pocket. As I have done before, I would be grateful. Do you catch my drift?"

"Yes, sir, I do. I'll get right on it. Don't worry about the trial." George stepped off the porch, mounted his horse and rode toward the sunrise.

*   *   *

Trying to stay out of sight, Frank moved about in the Sweetwater area. He watched to see if anyone followed him.

After dark, Frank ducked into the back of the Casper stores. He hid in the shadows. Moving at night, sleepless, he jumped at every sound. Hearing about the trial, he crept into the pasture behind the stable. After saddling his horse, he rode out across the prairie.

If I appear at the trial, I'm a dead man for sure. I have to stay out of sight. I bet that Henderson fella who does the dirty work for Bothwell is trying to find me. His thoughts ran over and over in a circle in his brain.

Days later, Tex Healy found Frank Buchanan in the Rattle Snake Mountains staggering and delirious.

"Frank, where have you been? What are you doing way out here? Why are you on foot?"

"Have you got water?" Frank's raspy voice asked.

Tex got his canteen and handed it to Frank, who took a long drink. "George Henderson shot my horse from under me. He likely hoped I would die out here without water."

"Why would Henderson be after you?"

"He works for Bothwell who is afraid I'll testify. I'm dead. Simple as that."

"Come with me back to my ranch. Rest up."

The men rode Tex's horse back to the ranch, where Frank stayed the rest of the day. He refused to talk. He sat and whittled until night and then he left without saying a word.

A short time later, George Henderson showed up at Tex's ranch. He knocked on the door and when it opened, he asked, "Is Frank Buchanan here? He needs to show up for the inquest."

"Nope, he's not."

George left without argument. Frank did not show up at the trial.

(Note: Months after the trial, Tex Healy found Frank's body rotting in the dry prairie land. He had been shot.)

THE TRIAL

CHAPTER
TWENTY-THREE

Town folk shuffled into the crowded room. From a side door, the sheriff ushered in the six cattle barons. They stood behind straight-back wood chairs on one side of a table. The sheriff stood at the end. Six men, the defendants, faced a wooden platform with a table.

The jury came in and stood behind chairs along the wall.

Judge Corn stepped onto the platform and sat behind the table.

"Everyone may sit." The Judge pounded his gavel. "The jury is now empaneled. Let the record show on October 14, 1889, Judge Samuel T. Corn opened the grand jury proceedings into

James Averell and Ellen Watson's hanging on July 21, 1889. Let the proceedings begin. Sheriff, please state the case for the grand jury to consider."

The sheriff rose to his feet. "Yes, your honor. I was informed by Tex Healy on Monday, July 21, 1889 in Casper that James Averell and Ellen Watson, both ranch owners, had been hanged on the Sweetwater River. I formed a posse and rode to Tex's ranch. Frank Buchanan, James Averell's cowhand and witness to the hanging, led us to where he said the hanging took place. We found two bodies swinging from the branch of a pine tree. We cut them down and buried them at Averell's ranch. Tom Sun was identified by Frank as one of the men who did the hanging. The posse and I went to Mr. Sun's ranch, and he confessed he was there and placed the other five men as having been there. They are all cattle ranchers. He identified Robert Galbraith, John Henry Durbin, Albert John Bothwell, who also admitted he was involved, along with Robert Conner, and Ernie McLean." The sheriff sat down.

The on lookers shifted in their chairs and whispered.

"Quiet!" Judge Corn hit his gavel on the table. "Thank you, Sheriff Watson. Now I want to hear from Tex Healy."

"Yes, sir, I'm here." Tex stood up from his chair in the front row of the audience.

"Do you swear to tell the truth?"

"Yes, sir, I do."

"Tell in your own words what you know about the hanging."

"I know nothing about the hanging, Judge. I know Frank Buchanan rode to my ranch with his horse all tuckered out. He said James Averell and Ellen Watson were lynched, and he saw it. He was riding to Casper to get the sheriff, so I went my own self and told the sheriff. After rounding up a posse, we went back to my ranch and Frank led everyone back to the awful sight I ain't never goin' to forget. Those two hanging in the heat for two days with flies and such. It was awful for sure."

"Thank you, Mr. Healy. You may sit."

"Now, I want to hear from Mr. Frank Buchanan, the eyewitness to the event."

Sheriff Watson stood. "Sorry, Judge. Mr. Buchanan disappeared, although he put up a five-hundred-dollar bond. We can't find him."

"Were there other witnesses?"

"Sort of. Ralph Cole, Jim Averell's nephew, but he died on September 9, 1889 of Mountain Fever."

"Mountain Fever, this far south?" asked the judge.

"Yes, sir. It happens. Just usually ain't fatal.

"Are there any other witnesses?"

The sheriff shuffled his feet. "Well, sir, there was John Crowder. He was one of the two boys who lived with Ellen Watson. However, we can't find him."

"And the other boy?"

The sheriff cleared his throat. "Me and my deputies can't find him either, but we're told he was last seen with some cattlemen and later died of Bright's Disease."

"Right's Disease is not a child's disease. Are you sure of this?"

"No, sir. But we can't find him."

"Do you have any evidence or witnesses about the hanging by one or all of the defendants?"

"No, your honor."

"I want the six men to stand."

The men got to their feet, and they all looked to Alfred Bothwell. Al smiled and nodded. He looked straight at the judge.

"The grand jury was told you men confessed to the hanging. Is the statement correct?"

The judge looked straight at Bothwell, suspecting he would do the talking.

"Not exactly, your honor. We did not confess to doing the actual hanging ourselves."

"You could not stop the hanging?"

"Oh, no, sir. We couldn't do that. The two nesters sort of slipped off the boulder of their own accord. No one pushed them or anything like that, your honor, and they were high up so we couldn't get near them."

"How did they get nooses around their necks?"

"I can't answer that, Judge. Their hands and feet weren't tied. Might be, it will remain a mystery."

Judge Corn narrowed his eyes as he stared at the men. A heavy weight of silence filled the room. After a long, sullen minute, the judge spoke, "Very well. You may resume your chairs. Sheriff, have there been any witnesses who have not been called or any evidence which has not been given in this matter?"

Sheriff Watson stood. "No, your honor."

"As there has been no direct evidence or direct eyewitnesses to this crime for the grand jury to consider, I dismiss the jury without a verdict. The defendants are released."

Mr. and Mrs. Countryman's mouths dropped as they stared at each other. While ranchers in the crowd cheered and whistled, farmers and smaller cattle owners jeered and shook their fists, they left and climbed into their wagon to face a long silent ride home.

Amid clapping on the backs, jeers and congratulations the spectators, the jury, and the defendants wound their way out the front door to the boardwalk.

Walking by the sheriff, Judge Corn said, "Sometimes, there isn't justice on this earth, I think this is one of those times. Fortunately, I believe there is a final justice, for if I didn't, I would hate my job."

LIFE GOES ON FOR SOME

Albert Bothwell

Striding into the Cheyenne Club, Albert Bothwell smiled as men came forward and offered their hands in greeting.

"Congratulations, Al. Becoming a member of the Executive Committee of the Wyoming Stock Growers Association is a fine honor indeed." Tom Sun shook Albert's hand.

"Yes. Now, I can get a few things through the committee that will help all the large cattle ranchers. I'm working to be the president of the Western Breeders Association someday. We need to keep our interest growing." Al strode into the smoking room and the men found their favorite chairs, letting Al sit first.

"Al, your men have been busy. They have taken down all the barbed wire fencing at the Watson's place and Averell's. They even moved some of Averell's buildings to the back of your ranch house," said John Durbin.

"Yeah, it's my land now."

"The law says it's public land. Are you going to file a claim on it?"

"Don't need to. It's my land. My cattle graze on it. No need to file anything." Al's voice rose, and he pounded his fist on his knee.

The room became silent.

*   *   *

In 1917 Albert Bothwell moved to Los Angeles.

"Your lawyers are here" said Alice as she ushered into the library two men in business suits and bowler hats. They put their briefcases on the desk where Al sat.

"Mr. Bothwell, the sale of your Wyoming ranch is in a terrible mess. We can't find any proof that you have a legal right to all the property you sold to the Sanfords. We'll have to renegotiate the sale of the buildings, animals, and land you do hold deeds to. The federal government is involved, and they will not let you sell public lands to the Sandfords."

"All right. Do what you have to do. My family and I enjoy living in Los Angeles, and I don't want to go to Wyoming to settle. I'm sick of ranch life and cattle. I've been making business deals in California. Now, go away, I'm busy."

(Note: It was discovered later that the gold mine Bothwell and the oil drilling investments did not exist, and only a few lots in the Town of Bothwell were sold. The Sweetwater Chief Newspaper began publishing in the town of Bothwell in April 1889. However, it lasted only a few months, as the Town of Bothwell soon did not exist. When it became obvious to John (Al's brother), the town would never prosper, he went back East and did not see his brother, Albert, again. All the investors lost their money, but it showed how clever Albert Bothwell could entice investors into his schemes.

Bothwell died March 1, 1928, at the age of 74 in Los Angeles and his family buried him in the Inglewood Park Cemetery at Inglewood, Los Angeles, California. The authorities reported, he died of Bright's Disease, which some people say Bright's Disease killed Gene Crowder so he would not testify against Bothwell, and chronic heart disease. Some people believed Mr. Bothwell was insane at the time of his death.

Robert B. Conner

A month after the inquest, Conner rode out on the range of his Lazy UC Ranch. Trotting his horse over to his foreman, Ordway, he stopped.

"Ordway."

"Yes boss. What brings you out this way?"

"Rustle no more cattle to add to my herd. The number stays as is. I'm selling the ranch, lock, stock, and barrel. Don't worry, the new owners will probably keep everyone on."

Ordway took off his Stetson and wiped his sweaty forehead and neck with his bandana. "Why are you doing that, boss? Is it cuz of the nesters hanging? That is over. You ain't got nothing to worry about." Ordway put his hat on and stared at Conner.

Conner shifted in his saddle and looked off into the distance. "No, of course not. I'm not worried about that business. It really had nothing to do with me. It was all Bothwell's doing."

"You ain't worried about what folks are sayin' you might have poisoned that Robert Cole fella with strychnine? You know they can't prove it. It was Mountain Fever that kilt him."

"Of course, it was Mountain Fever. I had nothing to do with his death. I want to go back to my hometown in Pennsylvania and see what it's like now. That's all."

"Okay, if you say so."

"I don't know who the new owners will be, but more than likely, they will let you rustle cattle for yourself. Still got nesters to blame." Conner wheeled his horse and trotted back to his ranch.

(Note: Mr. Robert B. Conner did not marry. He later lived in his hometown Mauch Chunk, Pennsylvania. By this time, he was a millionaire. After donating his money to many charities, he left his estate in trust to help the poor. On September 13, 1921, he died from heart failure at the American Hotel at the age of 72. He is buried in the Mauch Chunk Cemetery. The name Mauch Chunk is from the indigenous Lenni Lenape people and means Bear Mountain or Sleeping Bear, which refers to the shape of a nearby mountain. The town's name was later changed to Jim Thorpe.)

Mr. and Mrs. Countryman

Mr. and Mrs. Countryman owned the ranch where Ernest McLean confessed what he did. They never came forward with any information.

Dr. Benson

Dr. Benson who acted as the Coroner at the site of lynching. His real name was Joseph P. Riley. I could not find the reason he changed his name. After being incarcerated many times in Casper's jail for drinking, he started a fire to burn a hole in the wall to escape. The fire got out of control. People tried to shoot the lock off the door of the cell. Using a rake, they pulled out his burning body from the raging fire. He was dead.

John Durbin

Throwing down her beaded handbag on the dressing room table, Emma said, "John, I can't stand this anymore. Everywhere I go, people stare and whisper. And that darn awful Mrs. Clark said she didn't invite us to the last musicale because the weather was so damp, she thought it would bother your leg." Emma took the hat pins from her hat and put them on the dressing table.

"The dampness does bothers my leg." John sat on the bed and removed his shoes.

"Your limp reminds everyone about the hangings, and it proves you took part as you were shot in the hip. People want to forget. I want to forget."

"It was almost two years ago, and people may want to forget, but won't. You are right. So I resigned from my position as a Wyoming cattle inspector today. And I'm selling the ranch and our place here in Cheyenne. We will start over."

"Darling, really? How wonderful of you. Where will we go?"

"With the sale of everything, we should have plenty of money to start up more slaughterhouses, even beyond Denver. Might have a string of them in several cities."

"Wonderful, John. I love you." Emma kissed her husband on the cheek and put his shoes in the closet.

(Note: when John Durbin owned his ranch, he also had government contracts to furnish supplies to the Indian agencies. He parlayed this into huge profits. At the height of his years as a rancher, he was worth several million. His slaughterhouses were a tremendous success. After gambling away millions, he still lived comfortably. He was an active member of the Plymouth Congregational Church. His two daughters, Alice Durbin, and Mrs. Frank Benton, survived him. Dying at the age of 64, his family buried him in Fairmount, Colorado)

Robert Galbraith

"Well, my dear Ophelia, what do you say about our selling the T Bar B Ranch and taking our three boys to a place called Little Rock, Arkansas? My friend says he loves it there and says we should join him. With my money, I can start a bank and we would live a good life."

"Robert, do you want to sell and move because of what people said at the inquest? That is all over, you know. People will forget."

"Yes, darling, but I've been paying fifty cents to the ranch hands to file homestead claims in their names and any names they thought of to increase the size of the land for grazing. That land is deeded over to me. So, I'll get plenty of money." He fussed with his string tie around his starched collar.

"I know, my dear." Ophelia batted his hands away. "Here, let me help you. Why are you thinking about leaving here and going to Arkansas?"

"Do you remember when I escorted that scientist to look at the eclipse. It got me thinking there is more to this world than cattle ranching." He lifted his chin higher.

"What about leaving the Presbyterian Church in Rawlins? We've been a member for years and have many friends?" "I'm sure Little Rock has churches."

Ophelia studied her husband as he talked. She noticed he never made eye contact with her. *I sense desperation in him.* "Let's do it. We need a change. Tell me when to pack." Ophelia patted the finished tie.

Robert kissed her. "I love you." Robert linked his arm around hers.

(Note: Robert and Ophelia celebrated their fiftieth wedding anniversary in September 1920. Robert died at Pine Bluffs, Arkansas, at ninety-five.)

George Henderson

George Henderson was reputed to be the person who was contracted to kill the witnesses. No evidence connected him to any deaths. He did get instructions from Albert Bothwell to start the stories in the newspapers that Averell and Watson were thieves and murderers.

(George Henderson was shot to death on his front porch while bringing home groceries.)

Ernest McLean

Ernest walked into the bank. "Hi John, do you have a few minutes?" "Sure do, Ernest. Glad that trial stuff is over for you. So, what brings you into the bank today?" The two men shook hands over the banker's desk.

"I have a buyer for my EM Bar Ranch. They want to buy the property and the Durham milk cows and continue making butter, cheese and buttermilk. They'll run it just as I do."

"Why? You're doing substantial business. What will you do without the ranch?"

"I'm tired of all this cattle range business. I want to get out and go to Chicago. Can you handle the sale and make it as quick as possible.?"

"Sure can, but I'm sorry to see you go, Ernest."

(Note: I could not find where Ernest McLean lived after he left for Chicago.)

Tom Sun

At the front door of his ranch house, Tom halted the horse pulling the carriage. Helping his wife, Mary Agnes, from the buggy, he handed the reins to a stable groom. As soon as Mary walked into their home, she removed her hat and white gloves. After Tom hung his Stetson on the hat rack, he walked over to the liquor table and poured a whiskey.

"Is that how you're going to handle everything from now on?" Mary sat on a straight back upholstered chair.

"What do you mean? I'm celebrating. You heard the verdict. No witnesses. No one is charged. Life goes on as always." Tom took a sip and sat on the settee.

"Life goes on. It doesn't go on for the two hung on a tree. How are we going to face people? Everyone knows you took part in their murder." She fiddled with the gloves in her hands as a tear spilled down her cheek.

"Why are you crying? You never met them, did you!"

"No, But people will whisper behind our backs and point fingers. And we have children to think of. How can you sleep at night?" Mary Agnes paced back and forth in the parlor.

"The kids are young and don't know what's going on. I can sleep fine, thank you now that the trial is over. Besides, if anyone should lose sleep, it should be Bothwell. He brought the whiskey and led us to the Watson's and Averell's places and then the tree. I was there, but I didn't put the nooses over their necks or push them off the rock. They slid off. I think he planned the hanging all along. He wanted their land, and he got it. He was the master of it all.

"I have two gold mines worth twenty thousand and the Hub and Spoke ranch. Tom Sun's name means something around here. Something to be proud of I'm highly regarded. Life is good for us.

Note: Tomas de Beau Soleil, a French Canadian, was born on February 28th, 1844, in Canada and ran away at the age of eleven. The 1900 census report said he could not read or write. It also said he was born in Vermont and his name was Tom Sun, a U.S. citizen, which made him eligible to own land in the U.S.

He scouted at Fort Fred Steele with Boney Earnest whose full name was Bonaparte Napoleon Earnest. Buffalo Bill Cody of Wild

West fame scouted at the fort with Tom and Boney. Tom's wife was Mary Agnes (1856-1936). They had four children: Thomas Edwin (1884-1975). Anastasia (1887-1889), Adelaide Mary (1890-1983), and Eva Catherine (1893-1909). Tom died June 5th, 1909 at the age of 65 and the family buried him in Rawlins. His children and grandchildren ran the ranch and made it larger. His descendants were well regarded, and they raised Herford beef until the family sold it in 1977 to the Church of Jesus Christ of Latter-Day Saints. It is a National Historic Landmark and can be viewed by the public.

Thomas Watson- Ellen Watson's Father

After the hanging, Thomas Watson traveled to Rawlins and Casper to learn why his daughter was hanged. After being shown the condemning news articles and talking to people who were invested in the cattle industry, he became convinced his daughter was a rustler, and more shamefully, a prostitute. After returning home, he forbade any of his family to ever talk about her again. From generation to generation that view of Ellen Watson has been passed down. However, that is changing.

In 1989, her relatives met in Casper, Wyoming to commemorate her death. They erected a marker on what is now the Pathfinder Ranch. The inscription reads: COME YE BLESSED ELLA WATSON BETTER KNOWN AS CATTLE KATE JULY

2,1861 JULY 20, 1889 James Averell Mar. 20, 1851 July 20, 1889 both died by hanging at Spring Creek Canyon in Wyoming Territory, now known as the PATHFINDER 101 RANCH.

Over 130 years after her death, her descendants are learning the truth. She was not the infamous Cattle Kate and should not have been murdered.

Bob, Rosa, and Jim Rankin, and Mr. and Mrs. Countryman were people involved in the story as written.

Also Judge Corn, Sheriff Watson, Speers, Fetz, and Judge Emery, Mr. and Mrs. Fink were fictional characters.

Women were not allowed in the Wyoming Cattleman's Club except for special occasions.

I placed the fictional characters at the club to keep the story flowing.

LIFE DID NOT GO ON

James Averell

James Averell was born March 20, 1853, in Horton Township, Renfrew County, Ontario. His parents were John and Sarah Ann Averell. After the family moved to New York, his father died, and his mother remarried. James lived with his older sister and her family in Wisconsin. He attended school until he was 16 and worked in a sawmill for four years. His sister permitted him to join the U.S. Army as he was underage at 20. After James was discharged in 1876, he re-enlisted later in the same year. The events described in the book are correct about his time in the service, including his shooting of Charlie Johnson.

He married Sophia Medora Jaeger on February 23, 1882, and the circumstances of that marriage, her death, the child's death and burial are accurate.

His first log home in Wyoming Territory, he built for his family. After Sophia's death, he never went into the cabin. He sold everything, including the furniture, to Frederick D. and Robert C. Butler. After the lynching, they sold it to their foreman, Joe Sharp.

The two Butler brothers moved to Philadelphia. One brother stood in front of a full-length mirror and shot himself in the head. He did not leave a note. I do not know if his actions were related to the lynchings.

Governor Thomas Moonlight commissioned Jim as a notary public on February 11, 1889, and on June 29th of that same year, Jim became the postmaster for the Sweetwater Post Office and the Justice of the Peace.

He opposed the passage of the Maverick Law.

James (Jim, Jimmy) Averell died July 20, 1889. His friends buried him at his ranch, which later Albert Bothwell claimed was his. The land is now part of the Pathfinder Ranch.

Robert Cole

Robert Cole was James Averell's nephew and was about twenty years old when he visited his uncle. Shortly after the lynching, and before he could testify, he contracted Mountain Fever, and died. A rumor circulated, Bob Connor killed him with strychnine poison.

Ellen Watson

Ellen was married to Mr. Pickrell who beat her. She got a divorce and she moved to Red Wing and then Cheyenne and worked as a cook where she under took the care of the two boys, Gene DeCory and John Crowder. She married James Averell and had her land claim next to his. She was hung and buried with James.

Mountain Fever

Mountain Fever is a term for any fever which causes an illness and originated in the mountains. The symptoms are chills, muscle and joint pain, headache, deep pain behind the eyes, lumbar backache, nausea, and vomiting. The illness last for a couple days and then goes away but can return for another three or four days. At that time it was associated with adult males. If the adults are healthy, they usually recovered. It is now believed to be caused by a tick.

Bright's Disease

Bright's Disease symptoms are back pain, vomiting, fever, slight puffiness of the face due to an accumulation of fluid, which can distend the whole body, and sometimes severely restrict breathing. The urine is reduced in quantity and is of dark smoky or bloody color.

Today, it is not called a disease but acute or chronic nephritis.

The poet Emily Dickinson reportedly died of Bright's Disease as did Gene DeCory.

RECIPES

Salt Pork in Milk Gravy

Slice one- pound salt pork thinly. Dip slices in boiling water. Drain, then cover with cornmeal. Brown slowly in a skillet until cooked through. Remove salt pork to a plate. Add one chopped onion and sauté until golden. Then make milk gravy by putting 4 tablespoons of lard into a skillet. Stir in one-third cup flour. When mixture bubbles, gradually add milk. Season with salt and pepper. Return the salt pork to the gravy. If the gravy is too pasty, reduce it with a bit more milk. Serve with cornbread and greens.

Pork Snow Birds

Mix one-and one-half pounds of ground pork shoulder, one cup of uncooked white rice, and onion chopped fine, salt, pepper, and form into balls. Place in a skillet, pour in one pint canned or cooked tomatoes, two cups boiling water, and simmer two hours, keeping the skillet covered. You can also bake this in the oven in a covered casserole dish. Serve hot. Be sure the pork is thoroughly cooked.

Whipped Syllabub

This recipe is a variation of a recipe which first appeared in 1739 and has changed from almost all liquid to half liquid and a creamier top. It was common in the late 1800s. Considered being a dessert beverage.

Ingredients for the base:

Approximately ½ to ¾ cup of white wine per serving. (Some recipes call for Sack or sherry, Rhine White Wine, or Claret, but feel free to use another white wine or even hard cider. For a non-alcoholic version, try white grape juice or apple juice.)

About ½ to 1 teaspoon sugar per serving (you may wish to eliminate the sugar if you're using a sweet wine.)

Set the above ingredients aside.

Ingredients for the topping:

1 cup white wine or juice

½ cup sugar

Juice of 2 lemons (less if you desire a less-tart topping)

2 cups heavy cream

Garnish with grated nutmeg and a squeeze of lemon rind

Directions for the Topping:

Combine the wine or juice, the lemon juice, and a ½ cup of sugar in a bowl and stir until it dissolved the sugar.

Once the sugar is dissolved, pour in the heavy cream.

Whisk the mixture until it forms soft peaks or use an electric mixer.

Fill each of your serving glasses about half full with the base juice or wine, then top with the whipped cream mixer. Fill it to the top of the glass. Garnish with a bit of nutmeg and lemon rind.

(Note: I suggest you do not use sparkling cider as the carbonation pushes the whipped topping up and out of the glass and is messy.)

I made this with white grape juice and liked it. I am sure it is calorie intensive.

Scripture Cake

¾ cup Judges 5:25 (butter)

1 ½ cup Jeremiah 6:20 (sugar)

5 Isaiah 10:14 (eggs, separate the whites from the yolks)

3 cups sifted Leviticus 24:5 (flour)

¼ teaspoon 2 Kings 2:20 (salt)

3 teaspoons Amos 4:5 (baking powder)

1 teaspoon Exodus 30:23 (cinnamon)

¼ teaspoon each 2 Chronicles 9:9 (nutmeg, ginger, and powdered allspice)

(The Bible says spices, but printed recipes say nutmeg, ginger, and powdered allspice. The pioneer women may have thought the spices should be nutmeg, ginger, and powdered allspice, as these were the ones available to them. I could not find a Bible for the listing of these specific spices for 2 Chronicles 9:9 even going back to an old King James Version.)

½ cup Judges 4:19 (milk)

¾ cup chopped Genesis 43:11 (almonds, or pistachios)

¼ cup 2 Samuel 16:1 (raisins or figs)

Cream butter and sugar until light and fluffy. Beat in egg yolks, one at a time, mixing well after each addition. Sift together flour, salt, baking powder, cinnamon, nutmeg, ginger, and powdered allspice.

Beat flour mixture into butter mixture, alternating with milk until flour is just blended.

Beat room-temperature egg whites until stiff, fold into batter. Fold in chopped nuts, figs, and raisins. Grease and flour a 10 -inch tube pan. Put in the batter. Bake at 325 degrees until a cake tester or toothpick comes out clean, 50-70 minutes. Cool on a wire rack for 15 minutes. Then turn the cake out of the pan. When cool, drizzle with Burnt Jeremiah Syrup.

(Ten-inch tube pans were available to the pioneer women, but they also used 9X12 cake pans.)

Burnt Jeremiah Syrup

(Note: Burnt is the UK way of spelling burned) 1 ½ cups Jeremiah 6:20 (sugar)

½ cup Genesis 24:45 (water)

¼ cup Judges 5:25 (butter)

In a saucepan over low heat, melt sugar, occasionally stirring to prevent sticking. When sugar is melted, continue stirring and cooking until it is a deep golden color. Add water and cook, stirring until smooth. Remove from heat, stir in butter. Cool. Drizzle over cooled cake.

Garnish with Genesis 43:11 (almonds or pistachios and ¼ finely chopped Jeremiah 24:5 (figs)

(The cake is like a coffee cake, heavier than a regular cake, and it is dry. The Burnt Jeremiah Syrup helps moisten the cake.)

Wild Apple Maple Duck 1 wild duck (or 1 chicken)

½ cup raisins

3 firm apples, peeled and sliced into wedges

4 strips of bacon

6 oranges

Real maple syrup

Combine the apples, raisins and stuff into duck cavity. Place the duck in a roasting pan, cover the breasts with bacon strips (you can secure strips with toothpicks.) Pour strained juice of oranges and ¼ cup maple syrup over the duck. Bake at 350 degrees until done, basting frequently. Be sure you cook the duck or chicken thoroughly. Cover with foil if it's browning too fast.

Scalloped Tomatoes

Butter a casserole dish and preheat oven to 350 degrees. Layer sliced tomatoes (use sun ripened beefsteak tomatoes if you can) with sliced onions and soft breadcrumbs. Sprinkle with fresh thyme and pepper. Cover the top with sharp cheddar cheese, then sprinkle a few breadcrumbs on top. Bake 15-20 minutes until bubbly.

Quick Fruit Upside-Down Gingerbread

Butter your iron skillet or dutch oven and add a can of apple, or cherry, or peach, or blackberry pie filling, spreading it out evenly. (We've tried every fruit and prefer apples). Pour the ginger bread batter on top of the fruit and bake about 25 minutes in a 350-degree oven until the cake is done. If you're camping and using a size 8 Dutch oven, put some coals underneath and just a few on top of your pan. Check after 20 minutes. To serve, spoon out and top with freshly whipped cream.
Use the Gingerbread recipe below.

The Good Gingerbread

½ cup sugar
½ cup buttermilk
½ cup molasses
1 tsp. soda (dissolve in milk)
1 egg
1 tsp. ginger
¼ cup butter
½ tsp. cinnamon 1 ½ cup pastry flour

Cream sugar, molasses and butter. Beat in egg. Mix spices with the flour and add alternately with the buttermilk and soda. Pour into a buttered glass dish or iron skillet. Bake at 350 degrees for

25-35 minutes or until cake springs back to a light touch. (Or buy a gingerbread mix at the store.)

Vinegar Pie

1 cup water
1 cup sharp vinegar
3 cups sorghum
1/3 cup grated cracker crumbs or soda biscuit
½ cup butter 1
teaspoon nutmeg or 2 teaspoons lemon extract

Prepare standard crust for a two-crust pie. (These are now available in stores.)
Preheat the oven to 350 degrees F.
Combine the water, vinegar and sorghum and boil stirring for 5 minutes. Stir in the cracker crumbs and butter. Add the flavoring. Put into the pie crust and bake for 35 minutes or until crust is golden.

POSSIBLE QUESTIONS FOR BOOK CLUBS

1. What was the main driving forces for each of the characters?
2. Who did you like the most?
3. Who did you dislike the most?
4. Which character(s) surprised you the most in what they did?
5. Why were the early reports of the murders justified by the people of Cheyenne?
6. What about Frank Buchanan? Should he have testified?
7. What do you think about the characters in the Life Goes On section?
8. Should have James Averell and Ellen Watson sold their ranch?
9. Do you think James Averell should have been tried for killing Charlie Johnson?
10. Should Mr. and Mrs. Countryman have testified?
11. Do you think the role of the wives may have influenced their husbands?

REFERENCES

"What is Bright's Disease?" Yahoo Answers

Aldous, Jay A. "Mountain Fever in the 1847 Mormon Pioneer Companies"

Article adapted from Mr. Denardo Designed's information by Kidd Creative Powered by WordPress Article Titled "Sun Ranch Cabins."

Chandonnet, Ann, The Pioneer Village Cookbook. Native Ground Books and Music, 2010. https://en.wikipedia.org/wiki/JohnsonCountyWar

Franklin, Linda Campbell, 300 Years of Kitchen Collectibles. Iola, Wisconsin: 1997. Page 504.

Hufsmith, George, The Wyoming Lynching of Cattle Kate, 1889. Wyoming: Hight Plains Press.

Keen, Cindy K. "Double Lynching in the Sweetwater Valley" Wild West Volume 15 Number 2 pgs. 30-36 &74.

Lopez, Cindy. "Albert John Bothwell in the U.S., Find a Grave Index, 1600s-Current", Sept. 18,2012

McGraw, Eliza. "The Tragedy of Cattle Kate," Smithsonian Magazine March 12, 2018

Rea, Tom. "Covering Cattle Kate: Newspapers and the Watson-Averell Lynching." WyoHistory.org, November 15, 2014.

Simkin, John john@sparatacus-educational.com

Swell, Barbara. Secrets Of The Great Old-Timey Cooks. North Carolina: Native Ground Music, Inc. pages 30,32,45.

Todd, Tom. "Thomas DeBeau Sun." Find a Grave Sept. 26, 2002

Tusler, Kyle. "Honor Senior thesis" Rocky Mountain College. Spring 2013.

Walker, Barb. "Ellen Liddy Ella Watson." Find a Grave Aug.20, 2010.

Walker, Barb. "John Henry Durbin." Find a Grave March 10, 2009

Weiser, Kathy. "Legends of America" February 2020

Weiser-Alexander, Kathy. "Albert John Bothwell-Inciting the Johnson County War" Legends of America, August 2017.

OTHER BOOKS BY PATRICIA STINSON

Range War Legacy

Range War Legacy is fiction but is based on historical facts. There was a sheep and cattlemen's war in Crook County, Oregon before and during Theodore Roosevelt's presidency. The war affects the lives of many people but especially young Molly Langster. She saw the slaughter of sheep, the murders of sheep herders, and a dear friend. Everyone in the community knew Molly could identify the killers, but she never did.

A review by M. Pers

"It is full of tension, conflict between families, good against evil, and takes place in the 19th century. It's about the cattle/sheep wars and how people lived and died hard. The main character Molly tells the story so well, you can imagine yourself being there amid all the action. A very good fast paced story that deserves to be read."

And a review by Kathleen Marusak, editor

"This is a story of courage, love and loss, as well as the hatred that can brew between men and justice that will follow their resultant acts, whether for good or evil. The kindness of Molly, the heroine, and the truth and beauty of God's country shine through in every scene."

Slaves of Passion

In the 1850's, a pregnant, slave girl passionately wants her baby to be born free. The slave owner's son thinks he is the father, and he intends to sell the baby. A mountain man living with the Nez Perce, brings his pelts to sell. He stays at plantation for a few days and later thinks the unborn child is his. Yatima does not identify who is the father. This leads to a difficult, dangerous journey to get to free territory. The child is born and for two more generations the identity of the father entangles the lives of others. Deception, hatred, love, savage times are a part of the family and survival.

Author's website is https://www.patriciastinsonwriter.com

Author's blog is https://gogoreadgo.blogspot.com

Author's email is pstinson23@comcast.net Please let me know what you think of this book. All comments are welcome.

www.ingramcontent.com/pod-product-compliance
Lightning Source LLC
Chambersburg PA
CBHW060229030426
42335CB00014B/1378